1st Pres. - Oakland

15529

Library
Oakland S.U.M.

Rocks, Rivers

AND THE CHANGING

Earth

By The Same Authors

HOW YOUR BODY WORKS

YOU, AMONG THE STARS

HOW BIG IS BIG?

LET'S FIND OUT

NOW TRY THIS

LET'S LOOK INSIDE YOUR HOUSE

LET'S LOOK UNDER THE CITY

Ac 1018

J
550
S

Rocks, Rivers

& THE CHANGING EARTH

A First Book about Geology

by *Herman Schneider*

& *Nina Schneider*

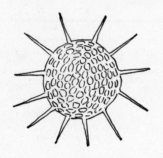

WITH ILLUSTRATIONS BY *Edwin Herron*

NEW YORK: *William R. Scott, Inc.,* PUBLISHER

Library of Congress Catalog Card Number: 52-7269

COPYRIGHT MCMLII BY HERMAN AND NINA SCHNEIDER. MADE IN U.S.A.

Table of Contents

PART FOUR
MAN AND THE EARTH

PART ONE
The Land Torn Down

A Leaf And A Stone

The story of the earth is in a leaf and in a stone; in a cloud and in the sea. The leaf was once a stone; the cloud was once the sea. The earth tells its story over and over again—the leaf will become a stone, the cloud will become the sea again.

The tops of mountains tell us that they were once at the bottom of the sea; and in the sea right now there are coral animals building land that will some day rise far above the sea.

The story of the earth is everywhere—in the shape of a pebble and the shape of a mountain, in the fresh taste of brook water and the salty taste of the ocean. You are part of the story, and so is the house you live in and the food you eat.

The earth tells a story that you can learn to read. When you know how to read it, you will see the earth in a new way. You will see it as it was long ago, as it is now, and as it will become many years from now.

Rivers To The Sea

Every part of the earth is changing all the time; no part is ever still. Every mountain, every brook, every mud-puddle changes from moment to moment. Some of these changes are so slow that they take millions of years, but others happen quickly. In running brooks and rivers, the changes happen right before your eyes. Let's look at a river and see how it changes.

Every river begins in the clouds. From high above the earth, rain clouds let fall the raindrops that come splattering down on the land. Where the rain falls on a mountainside, you can see a river beginning to flow.

There are all kinds of rivers, big and little, straight and winding, fast and slow. But no matter what kind of river it is, it begins as falling rain.

From Rain To River

To see how rain becomes a river you would have to climb a mountain and watch the raindrops as they strike the soil that covers the mountainside. You can't do that right this minute because you are probably not reading this on a mountainside in the rain. But you can make your own rainstorm on a mountain and see what happens when water falls on soil.

Make your own rainstorm and see what happens when rain falls on a mountainside.

EXPERIMENT. You will need a cup of water to be the rain. A rubber bath sponge will be the spongy mountain soil full of crumpled old leaves. You will also need a dinner plate.

Do this: over the kitchen sink, hold the dish in a slanting position and place the sponge in the dish. Then slowly pour all the water on the higher end of the sponge.

You will find that the water will soak into the sponge until it is filled. When it can't hold any more, you will see the water begin to trickle out of the lower end in a little stream.

Much the same thing happens when rain falls on a mountain. The rain pours down until it hits the soil. The soil soaks up the water like a sponge. When enough rain has fallen, the soil is like a full sponge. Water begins to trickle out in a little mountain stream.

6

A River Flows Downhill

The water trickles out of the spongy soil, always in a downhill direction. Sometimes it's hard to see the downward slant in places where the earth looks flat. But water finds even the smallest down grade and flows in that direction.

EXPERIMENT. You will need a big piece of wax paper and a large plate, cookie tin, or platter.

Do this: put the plate in the sink. Crumple up the wax paper and put it on the plate. Put some small thing under one edge of the plate, so that it will have a slight downhill slant. Pour a little water on the uphill end of the crumpled wax paper and see where it goes.

You will find that the water will work its way down even a very slight slope.

On the paper and on a mountain, water flows downhill.

7

In the same way the trickle of water on a mountain keeps working its way downward and then joins up with other trickles. Many trickles together form a stream flowing down the mountainside. This stream joins other brooks which have trickled down from other parts of the mountain. Lower down these brooks join and form bigger brooks. And soon the water from all these brooks flowing together is big enough to be called a river.

A River Keeps Flowing

But many rivers keep on flowing all the time, even when it isn't raining. Where does the water in a river come from on days when no rain falls? Here's a way to find out.

EXPERIMENT. You will need the same plate, a bath sponge, and a pitcher of water.

Do this: hold the dish and sponge in a steeply slanting position over the sink. Pour on just enough water barely to fill the sponge, so that little or no water trickles out.

8

Now quickly pour on a big splash of water and watch what happens.

You will find that the extra water will pour out at the lower end, but it will come out more slowly than you poured it in. It took you only a second to pour a great deal of water on to the sponge, but the stream will keep trickling for several minutes. A sponge can take in quite a bit of water quickly, and then let out a little water slowly for a much longer time.

Rainwater soaks into soil quickly and trickles out slowly.

In the same way, the spongy soil on a mountainside soaks up water. During rainy seasons the water pours in. In the Spring, snow melts and soaks down into the soil, too. The soil drinks up all this water like a great, tremendous sponge. Then, between rains and during drier seasons, the water in the spongy soil keeps trickling out of the soil and down the mountainside. That is why brooks and rivers keep on flowing even when it isn't raining.

9

Of course, the soil can't soak up an endless amount of water, and some kinds of soil hold more than others. Where the soil is deep and spongy, it is almost always full of water from past rains and melting snow. But, if there has been no rain for a long, long time, the soil may have no water left in it to trickle out. That is why some brooks and rivers do dry up when there is a long, dry spell.

Changes With The Seasons

Some seasons are dry and some seasons are wet, and a river changes with each change in the amount of rain or melting snow on the mountains. During the Spring, heavy rains and melting snow pour torrents of water down the mountainsides. The streams and brooks come tumbling and smashing down the mountain, rushing into the river. All that water makes the river rushing, deep, and powerful. It tears away at the shore line, cutting out chunks of it. It rolls big rocks along as if they were marbles. The more it rains, the higher the river rises in its banks. Sometimes it undermines tall trees along the banks and sends them swirling down, battering against the shore to dig away still more soil. In flatter places, the river, with all this extra water from the mountain, overflows its banks. It floods the nearby

10

fields and roads and drops sand and mud a long way from its bed. Later, when the flood waters get lower, they pick up twigs and leaves and other bits of soil and carry them away.

In a dry season a river changes all the time, too. It becomes lower and slower. The spongy earth has less and less water to trickle out. The streams go more slowly down the mountainside. The water stops tearing and tumbling. In some places it stands in the swimming holes and gets warm and muddy. The pools become shallow. Green water plants grow in these quiet pools, and frogs hide in the muddy bottoms. The roots of trees stick out along the dry banks. Everything looks dry. A river changes as the seasons change.

Other Changes

A river also changes from one moment to the next. As it flows along, a river picks up things and carries them along with it, so that it is never exactly the same.

If you wanted to see all the changes that take place in a river, you would have to put on a diving suit and go down and explore the bottom and sides of the river for several miles. But here is a way to find something about these changes, without using a diving suit.

EXPERIMENT. You will need a piece of cardboard folded like a long U, a handful of rough sand (such as builders and bricklayers use with little pebbles in it), a big pitcher of water, and a basin.

Do this: fill the U-shaped cardboard with the rough, gravelly sand. Hold the cardboard in a slanting position over the basin. Then pour water, a little at a time, on the sand at the upper end.

A flowing stream carries many things along with it.

12

You will find that, as the water trickles down slowly, it carries small grains of sand with it into the pan. But the pebbles which are larger and heavier will stay behind.

Now do this: quickly pour a lot of water on, all at once, so that you have a fast stream flowing.

You will find that both sand and pebbles will be washed off the cardboard down into the pan.

From this experiment you can see that when water moves, it carries things. When it moves slowly, it can carry along small light things such as grains of sand. When it moves quickly, it can carry heavier things such as pebbles.

A River Picks Up Things

A river is constantly changing because it keeps picking up all sorts of materials as it flows downstream. Where the water moves slowly, it carries along small, light pieces of sand and soil, grass-blades, leaves, and seeds. Faster moving water can carry larger pieces.

A river is busy picking up things all the time. What does it do with all these things? Do they just get carried along, or do they get dropped? Here's a way to find out.

EXPERIMENT. You will need a few cupfuls of soil that contain sand and pebbles, a glass jar with a screw cover, and water. (Keep these materials after you have finished this experiment since you will need them again for later experiments.)

13

Do this: dump the soil into the glass jar, add water almost to the top, and screw on the cover. Now shake the jar vigorously, so that the water moves very rapidly. What do you see?

You will find that all the soil swirls around when the water is moving very fast. In the jar, nothing settles down when you move the water rapidly.

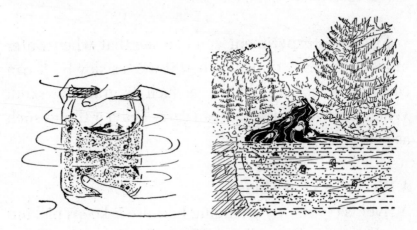

The faster the stream moves, the more it carries along with it.

Down Steep Mountains

Along steep mountainsides the water is fast-flowing. Just as nothing can settle in the jar, so nothing settles in this part of a stream. No sand or soil is left here. The rapidly moving water swirls and washes any loose material along with it. It rolls even heavy rocks down the mountain stream bed. The fast stream tumbles and crashes noisily among the boulders. The rocks and pebbles in the water smash against the river bed, cut-

14

ting it deeper all the time. Where the water pours down over boulders, it forms beautiful waterfalls and exciting rapids. Where the water, with its load of pebbles and rocks strikes the river bottom, it scoops out deep basins and washes away the sand. Such places are unexpected swimming holes and deep fish pools. Here, along the rapidly flowing part of the river, the water splashes and sprays, making the air moist and cool. This is often the loveliest part of a river.

In Less Steep Places

When the river flows through land that is less steep, it flows less swiftly. To see what happens, try this.

EXPERIMENT. Now shake the jar as fast as you did before. Then slow down a little at a time and watch what happens. (When you are finished watching, set the jar down and let the water stop moving altogether for the next experiment.)

You will find that when the water slows down, the heaviest pieces, such as the pebbles and small stones, settle to the bottom. But the sand and fine soil still spin around in the water.

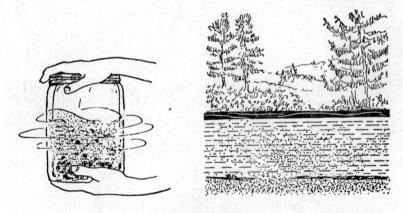

The slower the stream moves, the less it carries with it.

When a river flows a little more slowly and calmly, stones and pebbles are not carried along quite so swiftly. The heaviest ones settle to the bottom. The river doesn't tumble the biggest rocks, and they stop rolling. As the heavier things settle down into the river

16

bed, the bottom is gradually raised, and the river ripples along, gradually getting shallower and wider.
Along this part of the river are orchards and farms,
because the water soaks through the banks on both
sides of the river and moistens the nearby fields.

Through Hollows

Sometimes a river comes to a hollow, bowl-shaped
place. The water flows in and fills this bowl and a lake
is formed. You may not think of a quiet lake as being
part of a river that keeps flowing to the sea, but most

lakes are wide deep bowls of this kind—with a river flowing in at one end and overflowing at the other.

As you know from your experiments, when water moves slowly it drops most of the sand and soil that it has been carrying. In a lake, the water moves very

slowly, so that the lake bottom is covered with sand or mud brought down to it from a higher part of the land. Day by day, the bottom of the lake is filled in a very, very tiny bit. Little by little, the lake becomes shallower as it grows older.

18

Where the water flows out of the lake, it forms a river once again. If the land is steep, the river will rush and tumble on its way down to the sea, picking up more material to carry downstream. If the land is more level, the river will flow slowly and quietly. On its way, the river may join others to form a great river system, like the Mississippi or the Amazon, that flows for thousands of miles. But large or small, fast or slow, all rivers finally come to an end, and most of them end in the same way. They flow into the great ocean.

In Flat Land

Now if you look at the jar again you will find that as the water slowed down, more and more pieces settled to the bottom. If water moves slowly enough, most of the material it carries will sink to the bottom.

In the same way, as the river flows through flat land,

it glides along slowly and smoothly. Much of the lighter material that it has been carrying sinks, so that here the river bottom is sandy or muddy and the water becomes clearer. Here, where fine material is dropped all the time, the river bed is being filled up very, very slowly, and the river becomes more shallow. Here the river flows slowly and it does not have the power to cut and tear deep channels. It turns aside from every rise in the land, finding whatever downhill slope it can. Lily pads and rushes now grow along the edges of the wandering stream. Willows and alders line the low banks. The fields are well watered and a pleasant green. The landscape has a quiet look.

End Of The Line—River's Mouth

You have seen that slow-moving water drops the sand and soil that it has been carrying. This happens when the slope of the land changes from slanting to level. It happens too when a river widens out into a lake. And it happens again for the last time when the river reaches the widest place of all—the ocean.

At this last place, where river and ocean meet, most of the remaining material settles to the bottom. Year after year, sand and soil are brought down from mountains and steep places, and dropped at the mouth of the river. The bottom heaps up with it, and the river-mouth becomes shallower.

This heaping up of material at a river's mouth can matter very much to the people who live and work nearby. The mouth of the river may be a deep busy harbor where large ships sail in, bringing people and things. A good harbor needs to be kept deep. The sand and soil washed in by rivers must be dug up occasionally. This is done by special dredging boats equipped with machines that scoop or pump out the harbor bottom. The dredged-up material is loaded on scows and carried away to be dumped farther out in the ocean.

The filling up of a river's mouth is not always a nuisance. If the river contains much sand and soil, the material will heap up bit by bit until finally a new piece of land is formed. Such new land is called a *delta*. As the river continues to bring sand and soil from far up-stream, the delta continues to grow. New farm land is built up out of the river bed.

A rich delta has been forming at the mouth of the Mississippi River for thousands of years. By now, the river has built thousands of square miles of fine farm land on what was once river bottom. And the delta keeps on growing. A house built on the beach of a delta may in a few years be miles away from the water. It is impossible to make an accurate map of a delta because the land is being built up all the time. And all this building and changing is caused by a river flowing along at the quietest part of its journey!

A man-made city on a river-built delta.

The Moving Of Soil

When a river builds a delta, it uses borrowed materials for the job. The soil of a delta comes from hills and farms along the way. It is washed into the river by rain water and carried on downstream and dropped at the river's mouth. This moving of soil by water is called *erosion*. Wherever water flows over land, erosion is taking place. Every river in the world carries soil that was washed into it by flowing rain water. How much it carries depends on the heaviness of the rainfall and the condition of the soil itself.

Slow Erosion

When the rain falls on soil that is thickly covered with growing plants, very little erosion takes place. The

Growing plants help to hold the soil in place.

23

plants break the shock of the falling raindrops, so that the water strikes the soil gently. The plant roots soak in the water, hold the soil in place, and help to keep it from being washed away. On plant-covered land, erosion is a slow process. The soil moves very slowly into the river. The water is clear.

Fast Erosion

But in places where whole forests are cut down or where farm land is ploughed and left bare, the soil's protection is gone. When it rains on bare land, a huge amount of soil is washed into brooks and rivers and is carried down to the sea. In such places where there is no plant protection for the soil, erosion is speeded up greatly. This rapid erosion is a loss to everyone.

Where there are no plants, rain washes away the bare soil.

24

How Erosion Affects Us

Erosion is a loss to the farmer because it takes away the topsoil, the best part of the soil for growing crops. Underneath the topsoil is a poorer soil that gives poorer crops—smaller plants that bear fewer and smaller fruits and vegetables for feeding us.

Topsoil gives rich crops; poor soil gives poor crops.

Erosion is a danger to the people who live in farms and cities near a river. As the river bottom becomes heaped up with sand and soil, there is less room for the water to flow through the river bed. Then, in times of heavy rains and Spring thaws, the river may overflow its banks and flood the surrounding farms and cities. People are made homeless. The water supply becomes polluted by sewage and mud that washes into reservoirs and wells. The impure drinking water, the cold, and the damp and the crowding all spread disease.

When a river bed is filled by erosion, the river overflows its banks.

To protect themselves against floods, people have to build high river walls, called *levees*, out of concrete or out of heaped-up bags of sand. But heavy rains bring more mud and more floods. As long as rapid erosion continues, more soil is washed into the river, and the danger of flood remains.

Erosion is a loss to all of us, not only to the farmer but also to people who live in cities. When topsoil is washed into rivers and carried out to sea, its usefulness

to us is gone. There is that much less good farm land to feed us, and to provide us with cotton and other useful crops. With less and less farm land, we have to pay higher and higher prices for what the remaining farms can produce.

What We Can Do About Erosion

How can rapid erosion be stopped? It is not a simple matter that can be settled overnight. It takes a long time, and requires the help of every farmer and lumberman, of everyone who works with the soil. The job is directed by a special agency of our government called the Soil Conservation Service. They help us save the soil in two main ways—by protecting the soil and by controlling the flow of waters.

To protect the soil it must be covered. Where forests have been cut down and where land has been left bare, the soil is covered by planting young trees or

other green growing things that hold the soil, and sponge up water.

We also have to keep the rain water from flowing rapidly over steep and hilly land. Fast-moving water carries off a great deal of sand and soil, but water can be slowed down in several ways. Hilly land can be

ploughed so that the furrows will run level with the hill instead of running downhill. Conservation workers help the farmers plan their plowing so that the rain water stays in these level furrows and soaks into the ground instead of rushing downhill and washing soil away.

How Dams Help

Another way to keep water from carrying land away with it, is to build dams to hold back fast-flowing rivers. These dams keep the water from rushing wildly along steep places with every rainstorm and hold the water back so that it can be let out a little at a time throughout the whole year. Not only do dams protect the countryside from flood and erosion along river banks, but they can also supply water to farmers through the dry season.

A dam holds water back and helps prevent erosion.

In some places water from a dam is used to turn the water wheels of electric generators. The force of the flowing water makes useful electric power instead of destructive floods.

Dams have other uses besides helping to control floods. In many places a river builds up in the valley behind a dam and forms a lake which can be used for swimming, boating, and fishing. The water from such lakes often is also used to turn electric generators which make electricity for the surrounding area. In this way, fast-moving water can be controlled and released a little at a time to do useful work instead of bringing destructive floods.

By controlling the swift flow of water and by keeping the soil covered with growing things, rapid erosion of the soil can be prevented. Streams and rivers can flow peacefully and usefully through the countryside on their way to the sea.

Underground Water To The Sea

It's always raining somewhere. At this moment several thousand rainstorms are raining down on the world. Millions of gallons of water are striking the earth's surface. Every second, about sixteen million gallons of clean, fresh rain pour out of the clouds. Some of the water flows and swirls and cuts its way down mountain brooks and rivers that speed to the sea. But not all the land in the world is in the shape of mountains. The rain also beats on the level lands and low lands. Some of it soaks into the soft soil and seeps into the sand. What happens to this water? Where does it go?

Water Under The Ground

The rain water that soaks into the ground goes on a long strange journey through the dark, secret places of the earth before it reaches the sea. This water goes down into the earth to become part of a vast underground water system that is like a flowing, wavy lining under the earth's outer coat.

To explore this moving, changing, layer of water underground, you would need all kinds of digging machinery and perhaps a diving suit. It will be easier to see what we can find out by doing some experiments. Begin with this experiment and save the set-up for more exploration later in this chapter.

EXPERIMENT. You will need a large jar or glass baking dish. A fish bowl or aquarium will do even better. You will also need enough sand or gravel to fill the jar, and a pitcherful of water.

Do this: fill the jar with sand or gravel and then slowly pour water on top. Look through the side of the jar and watch the water sink down to the bottom. Keep pouring water until the level of the water is about two inches below the top of the sand.

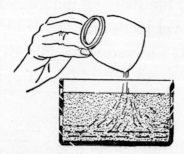

Now let's think about what has happened so far. We found that the water seeped down through the sand easily enough. It stopped seeping down when it reached the glass bottom.

We say that sand is *porous*—that is, there are little spaces, or pores, between the grains of sand, and the water works its way down through these pores. The water did not seep through the glass, because glass is *non-porous*.

The Water Table

Rain water falling on the earth soaks down through the soil, and even through some kinds of rock that are porous. It seeps down until it reaches rock that is non-porous, like the glass in the bottom of the jar. Here the water stops going down. Then as more rain water keeps seeping down through the porous layers, it piles up on top of the water already there, on the rocks that are not porous. As more water comes in, the level of this underground water rises, just as it did in the jar of sand. This water level under the earth is called the *water table*.

33

Where Is The Water Table?

Almost everywhere in the world there is water under the ground. If you dig down deep enough, sooner or later you will reach the water table. In some places it is quite close to the top. In some places you would have to dig several hundred feet through soil and porous rock. In some places you would have to dig through soil and drill through non-porous rock to reach water.

Even builders can't always be sure where the water level is. Sometimes, when the cellar for a new house is being dug, the diggers suddenly reach the water table even though the rest of the houses on the street have been dry. Where the water table has made a sudden upturn underground, the cellar hole turns into an unwelcome swimming pool that has to be pumped dry, and the sides and bottom made waterproof.

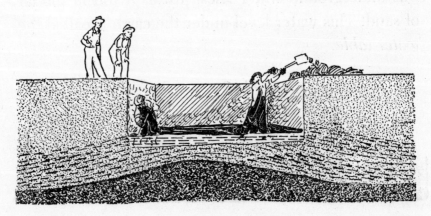

Using The Water Table

All over the world people have found ways of making use of the water table for a steady supply of water. You can find out how by going on with the experiment with the jar, sand, and water.

EXPERIMENT. Now you will also need: a spoon, and a tin can with the top and bottom removed.

Do this: hold the can upright and then wiggle it down through the sand, as if you were boring a hole. Work the can down until the top is even with the sand. Now use the spoon to scoop out all the sand in the can.

You will find that as you dig out the sand, water will come up in its place. When all the sand is out, the can will be filled with water up to the level of the water table in the jar.

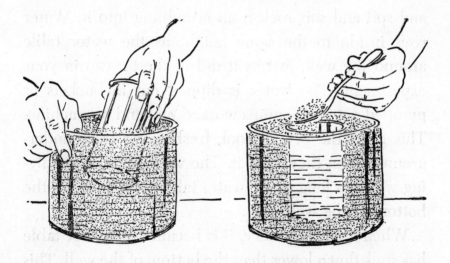

What you have just done is to dig a miniature well.

A Well

All over the world people get water from millions of wells that work in the same way. First a hole is dug down to several feet below the water table. Then the hole is lined with stones or tile pipe to keep the sand

If you dig a hole down to the water table, you have a well.

and soil and soft rock from crumbling into it. Water rises inside to the same height as the water table around the well, just as it did in the tin can in your experiment. The water is dipped out in buckets or pumped out with pumps worked by hand or machine. This gives the people cool, fresh water from underground when they need it. The well keeps on supplying water as long as the water table is higher than the bottom of the well.

When a well goes dry, it is because the water table has sunk down lower than the bottom of the well. This may happen in a dry season when not much rain has

36

fallen to seep through into the water table, or the water table may be lower because too much water has been used. Sometimes the well can be started again by digging the hole deeper in order to reach the lowered water table.

High Water Table

Even if you don't see a dug well, you can tell that the water table is not far below the surface of the ground. Where the water table runs close to the surface, you will find good, well-watered land, pleasant with farms and orchards. You can look at a shimmering, moist, green field and know that the underground water is gently wetting the plant roots.

A high water table brings plenty of water to growing plants.

There are many places in the world where the water table is very close to the top. Let's see what happens then.

EXPERIMENT. Do this: with your spoon, scoop out a bowl-shaped hole down to the water table in your jar.

You will find that the water seeps in just enough to make the sand sopping wet.

What you have done is to make a miniature swamp.

Swampland

In the same way, when the water table is very high, water seeps into the surface earth and makes it sopping wet. Such a place is called a swamp. In a real swamp, of course, there is more than just sand. All sorts of water-loving plants grow there, and the soil is often spongy and mucky from the rotting leaves that fall from these plants. This is not good farm land, but often deep woods and brush surround a swamp, and many kinds of wild things find a home in swampland.

Sometimes the water table is high and nearby land dips down. Can you guess what happens in places where the water table is higher than the land? You can find the answer in another experiment.

EXPERIMENT. Do this: dig down in the miniature swamp you just finished. Scoop out the sand until the bottom of the hole is two or three inches below the water table.

You will find that the water seeps in and forms a miniature lake.

Many lakes are formed in hollows that are lower than the water table. This is a different way of forming a lake from the one you read about earlier. In a lake formed by a river, you remember, the water flows through a bowl-shaped piece of land. In a lake made by the water table, the underground water seeps into the bowl-shaped hollow and fills it. Both kinds of lake are good for fish and fun.

Low Water Table

Sometimes the water table runs somewhat deeper below the surface soil. It runs high enough to keep grasses growing, but it is too far down for lush field or forest things. Water does not seep up to the plants above as generously as it does in good farm land. Here there may be grazing land and widespread ranches. Often the cattlemen must dig deep wells to provide water for their cattle.

Very Deep Water Table

There are some places in the world where the water table is very deep underground. Such places are deserts—great stretches of land where almost nothing can grow but prickly plants. The underground water in a desert is so deep down that it cannot soak up high enough to moisten the soil or the roots of the plants.

An Oasis

Even in a desert there are places where the water table comes close to the surface. Such a place is called an *oasis.* You have probably seen pictures of a desert oasis. This is a place where there is a layer of hard, non-porous rock under the sand. This hard layer keeps the water table close enough to the surface to be reached easily by digging a well.

Sometimes, when the water table is high enough, the water actually bubbles out of the sand in the form of a spring. Around these springs the ground is moist. Trees and green things can grow there. In desert regions, you will find villages located near an oasis because people were able to find water there. Palms and soft green things on the surface showed that water could be found below. Where there is water people can live and also take care of passing camel caravans.

Underground Lakes And Rivers

In some places where the rock layers are soft and the rainfall is heavy, the rapidly flowing and seeping water sometimes wears down the softer rock and carries bits of it away. In this way the water carves out hollow caves that become underground lakes and long channels that become underground rivers. Travelers come from far away to see the Mammoth Caves, Carlsbad Caverns, Ruby Falls, and other such lakes and rivers, where they can get a glimpse of the vast underground waterways of the world.

Sometimes an underground stream will flow out of the rocks and join a surface river. Together, the over- and underground rivers will then flow along on their way to the sea.

A Rock Sandwich

Sometimes the underground stream flows through a curious arrangement of rocks that might be called a "rock sandwich."

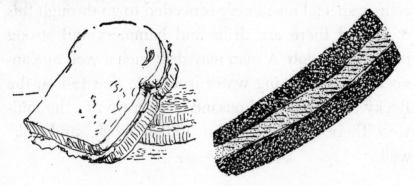

Sometimes rocks are arranged like a sandwich.

Think of a sandwich lying on the table with one end of the sandwich a little higher than the other.

Now think of the rock sandwich as being made of non-porous rock (not very tasty, of course), and the filling of sand or porous rock.

If you poured water into the sand or porous material at the higher end, it would seep down and flow out of the lower end. But you would not see any water anywhere else along the "sandwich" because the two layers of hard, non-porous rock would keep it from coming through.

Such rock sandwiches occur in many places in the world, and in some of them, water flows through non-porous layers for miles without showing above the ground. When people need a well in a place of this kind, they must dig and drill through the top layer of hard rock to hit the water in the "sandwich." Of course, special machinery is needed to go through this rock, and there are drills and hammers and strong pipes for the job. A man may drill such a well in Kansas and get drinking water from rain that fell on the Rocky Mountains a thousand miles away. In the midwest there are more than 15,000 "rock sandwich" wells.

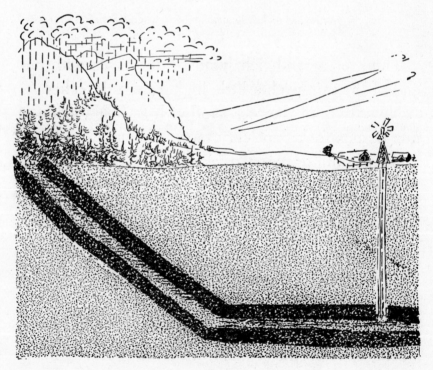

An Artesian Well

Sometimes when a well is drilled a lucky thing happens. The water spurts up out of the hole, in a fountain. This happens when the hole happens to be drilled at the bottom of a V-shaped "sandwich." In such a place, the water can be piped right up into the house without having to be pumped up, because the water from the high end of the "sandwich" helps to push the water up. This kind of well is called an *artesian well.* You may hear people call any deep-drilled well an artesian well, but only one where the water flows up without pumping is a true artesian well.

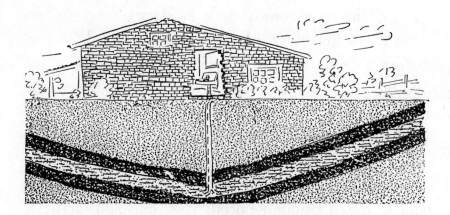

Out of artesian wells, deep-drilled wells, out of bubbling springs and plain dug wells, most of the people in the world get their water—all from the underground water table.

You And The Water Table

All over the world, the sweet, clean rain pours down from the clouds onto the land. It seems to sink into the deep earth and be lost to us. But it is not gone. It seeps beneath the sand and soil and porous rock until it reaches the hard, non-porous rock layer. On this hard rock bed, the underground water flows along. In some places, the non-porous rock is deep, deep underground, so that the rain water sinks hundreds of feet before it reaches its bed of rock. In other places, where the hard non-porous rock is close to the surface, the water table is close to the earth's surface, too.

Everywhere in the world, wherever you walk, there is water flowing beneath you on its secret way to the sea. You can't see the underground water as it seeps slowly down through porous rock and soil, or flows rapidly through underground lakes and rivers to the sea. But when you look at the surface of the earth, you can read some of the story of the hidden water underneath.

46

But whether it is high near the surface under the rich green fields or deep down low under the dry golden desert, everywhere underground water is flowing on its hard rock bed. And all the water comes from the rains and the snow. It falls on mountains and pours off into rivers that speed to the sea. And it beats on the level land and the porous places of the earth and seeps into the underground water system that also flows to the sea.

Precious Cargo

Wherever a river flows along, whether above ground or underground, it picks up material from the rocks and soil through which it flows. You can see some of these things, like sand, soil, and pebbles. But water also picks up materials that you cannot see in it—*minerals*.

What Are Minerals?

Almost all of the earth, except the plants and animals on it, is made of minerals. Minerals is a *name* for thousands of different kinds of materials in the earth. Everything made of rock or sand or cement or asphalt is made of minerals—many different kinds of them. The coins in your pocket—silver, nickel and copper— are made of minerals. And so are the aluminum pots in the kitchen, and all iron things, too. Shining gold and sparkling jewels are minerals. And you know of one mineral that you use all the time—salt.

When you sprinkle salt into your soup or into water, it dissolves. Other minerals, too, dissolve in water, though not so easily as salt. Rain water, as it trickles through the ground, constantly dissolves minerals out of rocks and soil. As it seeps through the ground, some of this water and mineral material is drawn up into the roots of plants, but most of it goes on its long journey to the sea.

Rain dissolves minerals out of rocks and soil.

Usually you can't taste the dissolved minerals which are in brooks or wells because they are in such tiny amounts. It's as if you dropped one grain of salt into a quart of water and then tried to find a salty taste in the water. But the minerals are there just the same, and here is a way of seeing them for yourself.

50

EXPERIMENT. You will need a very clean, dry drinking glass.

Do this: fill it half full of water from the tap. Put two pencils across the top, and then cover them with a sheet of cardboard, bent into the shape shown in the picture. This cover will keep dust from falling into the water.

Place the glass and cover in a warm place, such as on a radiator. The water will slowly evaporate (this may take several days or weeks), but the minerals will remain behind. They will form a pale white film on the sides of the glass.

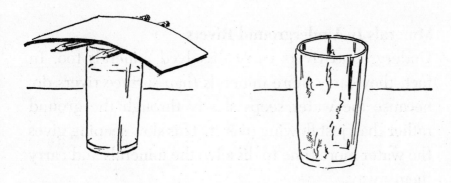

Now you know why you can't just rinse a glass in tap water, and expect it to dry clean and sparkling. The water evaporates, but the minerals remain on the glass and give it a cloudy look.

Some minerals can be an especial nuisance, because they prevent soap from doing its job of removing dirt. Water that contains lots of these minerals is called hard water. In towns where the water supply is hard, people have to use special hard-water soaps for washing jobs. Sometimes they install water-softening tanks. These tanks contain a chemical to remove the minerals that cause all the trouble.

It's not surprising that all ordinary water contains minerals. The water has to flow a long way from the place where it first reaches the ground as rain, on through brooks and rivers to the reservoir. On the way it has plenty of opportunity to dissolve minerals out of rocks and soil.

Minerals In Underground Rivers

Underground rivers carry dissolved minerals too. In fact, they carry more minerals than surface rivers do, because the water seeps slowly through the ground rather than just flowing over it. This slow seeping gives the water more time to dissolve the minerals and carry them away.

Water that has flowed a long way through the ground often has a special taste, because of the great amount of minerals dissolved in it. Some mineral water has a salty taste, some may taste bitter or iron-like, depending on what kind of rock or soil it has flowed through. If it has passed through ground containing sulphur, it may have the smell and taste of bad eggs.

For ordinary drinking, you probably prefer your

water plain, without the taste of eggs, salt, iron, or anything else. But some people do like these special flavors, or they think that mineral water is especially healthy. That's why bottled mineral waters are for sale in many drug stores and groceries. And that's why there are big resort towns, like White Sulphur Springs and Saratoga Springs, where people come to drink the mineral water that bubbles up from underground rivers.

Icicles Of Stone
Sometimes the water from an underground river seeps slowly down into an underground cave. If the water contains lots of dissolved mineral material, a very curious and beautiful thing happens.

Each drop of mineral-loaded water, as it seeps down to the roof of the cave, hangs there for a while. As it does, the water in the drop evaporates, leaving the minerals behind. The next drop does the same thing, leaving a bit of mineral clinging to the mineral from the first drop. Bit by bit, the minerals build down into a beautiful icicle shape. Such icicles of stone are called *stalactites*.

Sometimes, if the mineral-loaded water seeps just a bit faster, some of it drips to the floor of the cave. Then, as the water evaporates, it leaves minerals on the floor. Bit by bit, these minerals build up into upward-pointing shapes called *stalagmites*.

Stalagmites keep building *up*, and stalactites build *down*. When this happens for a long time, the two meet and form strangely shaped columns with curved sides. Sometimes they have beautiful colors because of the minerals they are made of. Sometimes, when the colors are especially beautiful and the caves are especially big, they become attractions for tourists from all over the country.

If you have ever visited one of these caves, then you know that the stalactites and stalagmites are very

hard, as hard as rock. In fact, they *are* rock, though you don't usually think of rock as something dissolved in water. Yet that's how these pillars and icicles came to be. They were made out of minerals that were once part of other rocks, perhaps hundreds of miles away. Flowing water dissolved the faraway rocks, bit by bit, carried them along in the form of dissolved minerals, and then built them up again, drop by drop, into the strange and beautiful rocks in the cave.

Of all the ways of the changing earth, this is one of the strangest—that rock should dissolve into water and then flow on, perhaps to turn into rock again, or perhaps to flow in a river that ends in the sea.

Cargo To The Sea

Most underground rivers do not end up in caves, but continue to flow toward the ocean. And almost all rivers above the ground end up in the ocean, too. During their travels, all rivers pick up sand and soil that they drop further downstream, but usually the salt and other dissolved minerals are not dropped. They remain in the water as it flows into the ocean.

Yet the river water that flows into the ocean is fresh water. It does not taste salty. But if you have ever gone swimming in the ocean and swallowed a mouthful, you know that ocean water is very salty indeed.

Why The Ocean Is Salty

Why is ocean water so much saltier than the river water that flows into it? Here is a way to find out.

EXPERIMENT. You will need: a drinking glass, ¼ glass of water, one heaping teaspoon of salt and a dish. Your experiment will work a little faster if you use a dark dish.

Do this: add the salt to the water and stir until all the salt is dissolved. Pour the salt water into the dish and put it on the window sill. Leave it there until all the water has dried out of the dish. You can speed up this experiment by putting the dish in a warm, sunny window or on top of a warm radiator. After the water has disappeared, examine the dish carefully.

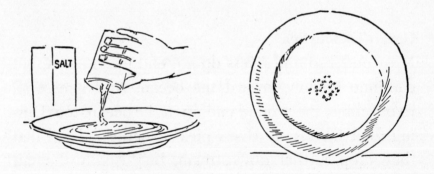

You will find that tiny white grains are left on the dish. These are salt grains, as you can prove by tasting a few. This is the salt that you stirred into the water at the beginning of the experiment.

This shows that when water and salt together are warmed, the water will evaporate, but the salt will remain behind.

family of monkeys hiding in a coconut tree, or send a family of picnickers running back for shelter. Perhaps it will fall on a thirsty wheat field and seep through to the water table beneath. Or it may once more fill up the spongy soil of a mountainside and then come trickling down as a tiny brook that joins other brooks to form a river that flows to the sea, thousands of miles away. Around and around it goes in its own continuous way. This never-ending path is called the *water cycle.*

Over and over again, water keeps making its journey from the clouds. The water you used to wash your hands this morning is millions of years old, and it has made millions of journeys to and from the clouds, and has traveled millions of miles. Perhaps, long ago, it turned a water wheel in a mill in Vermont, or it was churned into white foam by Columbus' flagship, or floated off the coast of Greenland, part of a huge iceberg, or shone as dew on a lilac leaf. It may have pushed a few grains of sand on to the banks of the Nile River in Egypt, or dripped off Abraham Lincoln's hat as he walked alone in the rain. You might have rolled it into a snowball or seen it steam out of a pot of soup. It might have been in the mud puddle your dog played in last week. But each time, the warm sun lifted it, and made it pure, and sent it up into the clouds, ready to fall again, clear and fresh, upon the earth.

Whether it flows over the ground in rivers and lakes or runs through rock passages and caves underground, water travels the same journey over and over again. It falls, it flows out to the sea, the sunlight lifts it up into the clouds, it pours from the clouds onto the earth and into the earth, and flows out to the sea again. It is never still. Over and over, water falls and rises—from the clouds to the clouds—forever freshening the thirsty earth in its endless journey.

Mountains Unmade

Water swirls and splashes and rivers are never still. But mountains never seem to change. You read about explorers struggling across the Rocky Mountains a hundred years ago, and those same mountains are still there. The narrow passes are still too perilous to cross in Winter. Patrols are needed to warn of ice and snow on the Donner Pass between Nevada and California, where so many pioneers and gold-seekers lost their lives long ago. But though they seem so very lasting, mountains constantly change.

You already know about one mountain changer. Water! You saw that moving water could carry along sand, sharp bits of split-off rock, and other materials, if it moves fast enough. The water that flows swiftly down a mountain brook, with these sharp pieces in it, works like a giant saw or like very sharp sandpaper.

The water cuts deeper and deeper grooves in the

brook's path, so that deeper and deeper cracks and notches are formed. The water files away at the rock, cutting out bits of it all the time, until the whole mountainside is covered with scrubbed-out wrinkles and cracks.

Day after day, water files away at the cracks and notches in rock. Finally, a piece is split off and swept away. A piece of mountain has been worn away and carried down. Bit by bit ravines and gorges are carved out of the mountainside. Inch by inch, the rushing brooks cut down the huge mountain.

High Land Is Cut Down By Water

Water can also carve high, level land into the shape of mountains. This is happening in many parts of the world, and the largest example of it is in this country, in the Grand Canyon of the Colorado River.

Some day, flowing water may cut down and across the high rocky land, until there is no longer a Grand Canyon, until all the land is cut down to the level of the sea. Not only in the Grand Canyon, but wherever rivers flow, land is being cut down.

Long ago the Colorado River flowed over high level land.

Then, as time went on, the river cut a valley into the land.

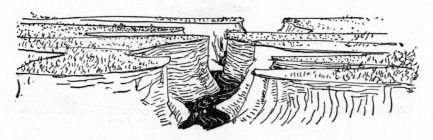

The river cut the valley deeper and deeper.

Now the same river is a mile below where it started.

Many years from now the sides may be worn away.

The high land may become rounded and worn down.

Until it again becomes a flat, low plain.

Rivers Of Ice To The Sea

You know about the work of running water as it chops down mountains and wears away high lands. But did you know that there are other kinds of rivers which also carve down and carry away the land? These are rivers of ice.

Most rivers begin as falling rain, but a river of ice begins as falling snow, high up on mountains where it is cold most of the year. The snow falls and piles up, and more and more snow piles up on top of that.

A river of ice begins its journey on a mountain top.

If enough snow is piled up, the bottom layers are squeezed so hard that they turn into ice, just as you can turn a snowball into an ice ball by squeezing hard enough. Still more squeezing does something to the layers of ice. Here is a way to see what happens.

65

EXPERIMENT. You will need: 6 ice cubes, 2 small flat plates (of the same size), and 4 heavy books.

Do this: rest each plate on 3 ice cubes. Place the books on top of one of the plates. See which ice cube set-up first melts completely.

You will find that the ice cubes under the books melt sooner. This is because they were squeezed harder than the others that had only the plate resting on them.

In the same way, in a river of ice, the bottom layer of ice with the great weight of snow pressing down upon it, melts slightly, just enough to become slippery. When it does, the huge mass of ice and snow on the mountainside begins to slide, very, very slowly. It becomes a slow-moving river of ice, called a *glacier*.

The Work Of A Glacier

A glacier keeps sliding downhill all the time. At its upper end it is fed by snowfalls, as an ordinary river is fed by rainfalls. And just as a river scours away the land through which it flows, so does a glacier. As it slides along, the ice picks up sand, pebbles, and even huge boulders, and it pushes them downhill, crunching and grating them under enormous pressure and scouring and scratching away at the mountain underneath. Year after year, the hard, rocky mountain is ground down by this river of ice.

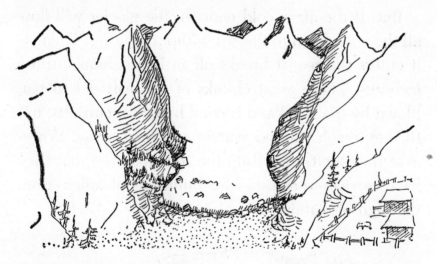

The glacier with its load of rocky material keeps sliding downhill until it reaches the end. The end of a glacier may be part way down the mountain, where the air is warm enough to melt the ice and snow. Then the melted ice and snow will just trickle on downward, leaving the rock material it has been carrying heaped up behind.

As the glacier melts, it leaves behind it the rocks it carried.

But, if the air is cold enough, the glacier will flow all the way down to the sea without melting. Then, as it enters the sea, it breaks off in huge chunks called *icebergs*. These great chunks of ice drift out to sea, blown by the wind and carried by ocean currents, until they reach warmer waters and melt away. Wherever they melt, they drop the rock material that they have carried—sometimes for hundreds of miles—from the high mountainsides.

There was a time, thousands of years ago, when the earth was much colder than it is now. Glaciers covered Canada, a large part of the United States, and most of Europe. The glaciers were so wide and deep that they became one vast sheet of ice which was over ten thousand feet thick. This great mass of ice left its story written in its path.

As these great, slow-moving rivers of ice inched their way downhill, they scoured the land, digging out valleys, leaving scratches and grooves in the rocks, as if a giant comb had been scraped over the mountains. The marks can still be seen on rocks over which the glaciers moved.

Where the ice melted, it dropped the rocks and sand it had carried along, perhaps for thousands of miles. Nowadays you may come upon a huge boulder that seems to be completely out of place, jutting up out of the land. If it looks quite different in color or grain from the other stone nearby, you can be sure a melting glacier left it there. Most of the rocks scattered through the fields of New England were brought down by glaciers that melted and left them behind. These glacial rocks made farming hard for the farmers who tried to plough the soil thousands of years later.

Glaciers changed vast stretches of land by heaping up materials they brought down from the mountains. In this way they filled up lakes, blocked up river beds, and sometimes even built new land out in the water. The big stretch of land called Long Island, over one hundred and fifty miles long, is made of material that was pushed along by the giant snow-plow action of a glacier and was then left in a heap by the melting ice and snow.

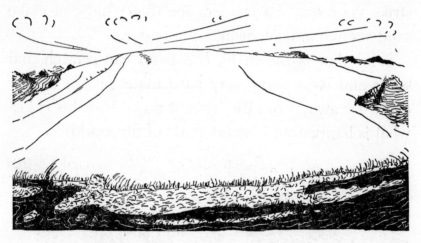

Thousand of years ago, a glacier built Long Island.

Glaciers have made many changes in the earth's surface. They have chopped down mountains and scattered the pieces far and wide. Wherever glaciers flow down a mountainside, the mountain is being worn down and carried to the sea.

Wind Cuts Down Mountains

When you walk along a sandy place on a windy day, you can see the sand lifted by the wind and swirled about. You can feel the sting of the sand grains as they

strike your skin. So you can see that wind can make sand scratch and scour like sandpaper.

Sand that is blown by the wind can scratch and scour and wear away very hard materials. In time it can wear away even the hardest rock. And this is just what is happening in many parts of the world.

In the Western desert, strange shapes are carved out of stone. Bit by bit, over thousands of years, hills and mountains have been worn away by the wind-blown sand. The strong wind and the sharp sand together have chiselled sculptures in the rock that tell a clear story of the wearing away of the mountains of the world.

Sunlight Cracks Mountains

Perhaps when you were out in the country you went for a walk along the base of a steep mountain. You may have noticed a large pile of rocks and boulders heaped at the bottom. These huge chunks all came from the sides and top of the mountain. They were pried off and cracked away, not by dynamite, not by powerful drills, but by the force of water and wind and by sunlight.

It seems hard to believe that something solid and heavy and hard like rock can be cut down by sunlight —something that you can't even hold in your hands.

If you wanted to see how the sun's heat cracks a rock, you would have to wait patiently for a long time, but you can speed it up by using the heat of a stove instead.

EXPERIMENT. You will need: a stove with a broiler and about 10 large pebbles.

Do this: put the pebbles on the broiler tray or in a flat pan. Put the tray full of stones as near to the broiler flame as you can. Turn on the broiler flame full and leave for a few minutes.

You will probably find that, in a minute or two, you will hear loud pops as pieces of the pebbles crack off.

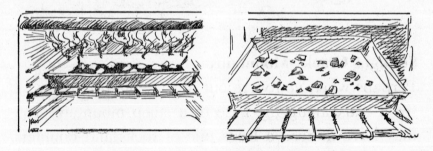

Here you see what heat can do to rocks.

You may have seen the same thing happen to stones that line a campfire spot. This happens because rocks, and most things, get larger or expand when they are

74

heated. The outside of the pebble was heated, so it expanded. But the inside, which was hardly heated at all, expanded very little.

A rock mountain is heated by the sun all day long. A stone in the sun doesn't get as hot as the pebbles in the oven, but the sun has been shining for a long, long time. Day after day, the heat keeps striking the sharp ridges and high bare peaks that jut up into the sunlight. Bit by bit, they expand, and finally they crack away. The mountain is left just a little bit shorter, and a little less sharp. The pieces of rock that split off from the mountain go clattering down to the bottom. Perhaps you have ridden along a road close to the base of a mountain and seen the sign "Danger! Fallen Rocks." Some of those rocks are hurled down by the action of the sun's heat. The high, stony mountain peaks are slowly being carved lower and rounder by the soft, warm sunlight.

Freezing Breaks Rock

Cold cuts down mountains in another way, by freezing water in the cracks in the rocks. You've probably seen a frozen bottle of milk with the cap pushed up an inch or two out of the bottle. When milk freezes it expands and needs more room. Water also expands when it freezes. When water changes to ice, it expands and needs more room. As it expands it can push very powerfully. You can see how powerfully by doing this experiment.

EXPERIMENT. You will need: two small bottles with screw tops, and water.

Do this: fill one bottle with water, right to the top. Screw the covers tight on both the brimful bottle and the empty one. Put them in the freezing compartment of a refrigerator. After an hour or so, look at the bottles.

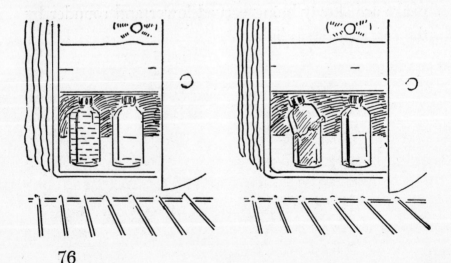

You will find that in one bottle the water has changed to ice, and that the bottle has cracked. The empty bottle did not crack because there was no water in it to expand and split it open.

It takes a powerful push to crack a glass bottle from the inside. When water expands as it changes to ice, it pushes with great force.

The same thing happens during cold weather on a rocky mountainside. In the daytime, water from rain or melting snow flows into cracks and pockets in the rock. At night, when it gets very cold, this water changes into ice and expands, cracking off chunks of rock that add to the heap at the bottom of the mountain.

LIBRARY

Plants Split Rock

Plants have a part in breaking rock. Sprouting seeds, as they swell up with moisture, are amazingly powerful. To see how powerful they can be, try this.

Experiment. You will need: one package of whole dried beans and a screw-top bottle full of water.

Do this: cram as many beans as possible into the bottle (some of the water will be forced out). Screw the bottle cap on tight and let it stand overnight in a warm place.

You will find that the beans, which are seeds, will swell as they begin to sprout. By morning they will probably have swelled so much that the bottle will be cracked open.

Who would think that little seeds could have so much power?

The power to crack open the bottle came from the sprouting seeds. And in the same way rocks can be split apart by seeds that fall into a notch or crack in the rock and then begin to sprout. The roots of a tree that began as a small seed, can crack apart quite a

78

large piece of rock. Many seeds all up and down the mountainsides work together to crack the mountain down.

The roots of a growing tree can break huge rocks.

Plants Change Rock

Did you ever look at a big rock closely? Here and there, on the rock, you will often find flat grayish-green or grayish-blue plants, called *lichens.** They look something like moss. Some lichens are so tiny they seem only like colored fuzz on the rocks. Some are larger. But they all have a special way of being able to live on rock.

* Pronounced *li'ke-ens.*

All growing plants need certain minerals that are in the earth. Most plants get these minerals through their roots from the soft soil. You know that these minerals were dissolved out of rock and soaked into the soil by rain water, and that most plants take up their necessary minerals with water.

But lichens have a harder job. They have to get their nourishment out of the solid rock. To do this, the lichens ooze out special juices that make the rock soft and crumbly. Then rain water is able to dissolve the minerals in the rock so that the lichens can get them. As the lichens work at getting their minerals, they start the breaking down of rock on its way to becoming soil.

If you can find a piece of rock with lichen on it, pull away a small piece of the plant and look at the exposed rock. You will see that it is slightly crumbly. Scratch it with a fingernail or knife, and you will find that it is softer than the part of the rock on which no lichens are growing. Wherever you see lichens, you are looking at rock being changed into soil.

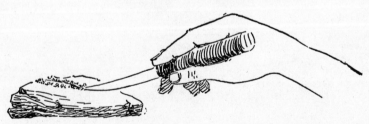

Even the tiny plants that grow on rocks help make soil.

What Is Soil?

When you take a walk in the country, you don't usually walk on chunks of rock. Occasionally you see rocks jutting out of the ground, but most of the earth's rocky crust is covered by soil and by plants growing in the soil. What is soil? How did it get there? You can find out by doing a simple experiment.

EXPERIMENT. You will need: a small glass jar with a screw top and some ordinary garden soil.

Do this: pour a handful of soil into the jar and fill the jar with water. Screw the top on and shake the jar. Then let it stand for a minute or two.

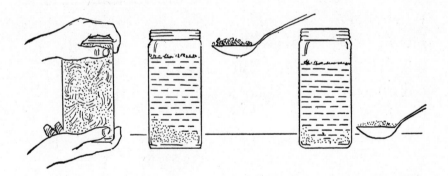

You will find that most of the material will settle to the bottom, but some of it will remain afloat on the top.

Now do this: skim off the floating material and examine it.

You will find that it is dark and soft. If you examine it closely you will find that it is made of crumbled bits of plant material—old dead roots, stems, and leaves.

81

Now do this: pour off the rest of the water and examine the material that sank to the bottom.

You will find that it consists of grains of sand and small pebbles—in other words, bits of broken-up rock.

Soil, then, consists of plant material and rock material. The plant material is simply the crumbled remains of the plants of last year and the year before, and so on back for many years. Rock, bare rock, began to be broken apart by heat, cold, rain, and snow. Lichens grew on some of that rock. They poured their juices into the bare rock, softening it a bit at a time until it crumbled away. Then other plants were able to grow in the mixture of crumbled rock and old lichens. When these hardy plants died, they broke up into bits of twigs and leaves that became part of the soil mixture. In this softer soil, more plants grew, and rotted into the soil to become still more soil.

Gradually, bald, rocky land was softened by weather and water, by plants and sunlight. Slowly, slowly, grain by grain, rock has crumbled into a thin mantle of rich soil. This coat of soil is shallow—only a few feet deep at the most. Yet, out of this shallow soil that once was rock, grow all the plants that feed us, all the green covering of the earth.

Changing Rock

Rock is everywhere in the world, and everywhere it is being changed. High up on the mountainsides, rock is split by the heat of the sun and cracked apart by freezing water. It is rolled and crushed by rivers of water and rivers of ice. It is crumbled by lichens and dissolved by flowing water. Over countless centuries, rock is turned into soil everywhere in the world.

But the journey of the rock is not ended. It is never ended. In every tiny part of every living thing are minerals that once were rock that turned to soil. These minerals were drawn out of the soil by plant roots, and the plant used them to form leaves and stems, flowers and fruits. When the plant was eaten by an animal, these same minerals became part of the animal. And still the journey of the rock is not ended, for nothing in the world remains unchanged forever.

A rock is not always a rock; a rose is not a rose forever. The fresh crisp apple that you may eat today is as old as the hills. And when you eat it, a tiny bit of those hills becomes part of you.

Just think of what that apple may have been before it became part of you! Once it may have been in the autumn leaves that fell and crumbled into the soil near the trunk of the apple tree. Years before it may have been in the shell of a robin's egg. And once it may have been part of a stalactite in some dark underground cavern. Perhaps for a short while it sailed high over the earth in a butterfly's wing. Long ago, it may have been in a kernel of corn planted by an Indian.

The things of the world are formed again and again, out of the same materials of the earth. Nothing is lost. Over and over, these earth materials have been part of many things in many places. Today, when you eat the apple, these parts of the earth become part of you who are part of the world.

The Land And The Sea Meet

At the coastline, where the land and sea meet, nothing is still. Rivers pour down with their cargo of soil and dissolved rock into the restless sea. You have seen that high land is hewn down to low land by many forces. And now, at the meeting place between land and sea there is another force that batters the land. Along the water's edge, waves roll in and beat against the shore, changing the coastline.

If you have ever wondered how waves are made, try making a few yourself. Next time you take a bath, sit quietly until the water is smooth and calm. Then blow along the surface of the water. You will see tiny

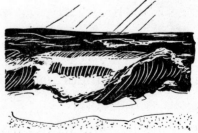

waves set up. The waves in the ocean or in a lake are made in the same way, by the action of the wind blowing over the surface of the water.

As they beat against the shore, night and day for thousands of years, waves cause many changes in the land. Some of these changes can be seen happening, while others take a very long time.

Pebbles Into Sand

If you have ever walked on a pebbly beach with bare feet, you must have wished that all those sharp pieces of stone could be turned into smooth sand. Walk down to where the waves are beating against the shore, and you can see your wish being granted.

As each wave topples over and smashes against the pebbles underneath, it sends them clattering one against the other. The sharp points and edges of the pebbles become worn away, leaving them smooth and round. More smashing and clattering, and the rounded pebbles are cracked apart into smaller and still smaller pieces, until finally everything is worn down to tiny grains of sand.

Of course, the waves don't grind the pebbles into sand overnight. To get a slight idea of how long it takes, try the following experiment.

EXPERIMENT. You will need: an empty tin can with a top, a handful of large pebbles, and a sheet of dark paper or cloth.

Do this: wash the loose sand off the pebbles. Dry them and put them in the can. Shake the can vigorously up and down one hundred times. Now pour the pebbles onto the paper.

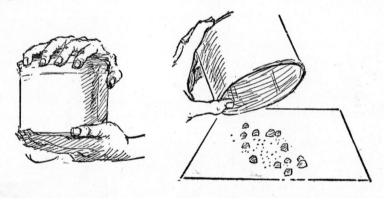

You will find that a few dozen sand grains have appeared among the pebbles.

What does this prove? When you shook the can one hundred times, you gave the pebbles more of a pounding than the waves give them in an hour. Yet you

87

chipped off only a few dozen or so sand grains. How long do you think it would take to turn the pebbles entirely into sand? To give you an idea of how long, consider that a handful of medium-sized sand contains about twenty-five million grains!

Of course, some waves are stronger than others, and some pebbles are made of softer rock than others. And seashells are still softer and crumble into sand more quickly. For these reasons you can't really tell exactly how long it will take for the waves to turn that uncomfortable, pebbly beach into soft, smooth sand. However, to be on the safe side, come back in about fifty thousand years.

Waves On The Rocky Coast

Turning pebbles into sand is not the only work that waves do. Along high, rocky shores the waves keep beating constantly against the rocks until they have worn away hollow places along the water line. This leaves the rock above the water sticking out in a kind of shelf. The waves keep wearing away the rock underneath until finally, with nothing to support it, the shelf comes crashing down to form a heap of rocks at the shore line.

A rocky coast doesn't remain like that forever. The continued pounding of the waves gradually breaks the boulders into smaller rocks, and then into pebbles, and finally into sand.

The Ever-Changing Coastline

High rocky cliffs are cut down. Sharp points are beaten off. Pebbles and seashells are thrown up by the waves, and ground down into fine sand, along with the rocks broken off the cliffs. At the same time, rivers come into the ocean and drop their cargo of sand and soil. Every moment of the day and night the rivers keep pouring into the ocean, building up deltas and filling up bays and harbors. Bit by bit, the coastline is changed by the rivers that flow into the ocean and by the ocean itself.

Working together, year after year, the ocean and the rivers gradually change a rugged, jagged coastline into a smooth, straight one.

Does It Matter?

Does it matter whether a coastline is wrinkled or straight? To the people who live and work nearby it matters very much. Where the coastline is wrinkled, there are sure to be good, safe harbors. The harbors are good because they are deep enough for large ships to sail in, and they are safe because the curving land on either side protects the ships from strong winds. Where a coastline is straight, the bays are very few, the bottom is usually too shallow for large ships to come in close, and there is no protection from storms. A good harbor usually means that many ships come, bringing goods, business, and easy communication to and from other countries.

Along every coast, where land and water meet, there are constant changes taking place. The waves pound endlessly on the shores and beaches, and every wave changes the world.

PART TWO

The Sea Filled In

The Ocean

Everything seems to be headed on a one-way trip down to the ocean. Rivers flow down into the ocean. Mountains are worn down by rivers that carry them, piece by piece, down into the ocean. Soil and minerals are carried down into the ocean. And along every coastline in the world, the waves keep chopping away at the land and dragging the broken pieces down into the ocean.

Well, is the ocean a bottomless pit that can keep endlessly swallowing the land that pours into it? How deep is it, and how wide, and where does it end?

Let's Look At The Ocean

All you have probably ever seen of the ocean is the top
—unless you are a good diver, in which case you may
have seen it a few feet under the surface. But the ocean
is of course much deeper than that. In most places it is
over two miles deep. That would seem quite deep if

you tried to reach the bottom, but actually the ocean
bottom is only a rather shallow scoop in the huge earth.
The scoop is not smooth and level; so there are many

96

underwater hills and valleys. Some of the valleys are as much as seven miles below the surface of the water. And some of the hills are so high that their tops jut up above the water. Wherever the tops of these mountains reach up above the water, there are islands in the vast ocean.

The ocean has a bottom and it has a top, but where does it end? Does it end along the coast of Europe, or Asia, or the North Pole, or where? In what direction would you sail to find the end?

You could never find the end, because the ocean has no end. It is one big ocean that goes all around the world in every direction. And because the one ocean goes all around the world, it is possible to sail to any harbor. No matter which way you sailed or which land you came to, you could sail around that land into another part of the world.

Even though there are many ocean *names*—the Atlantic, the Pacific, and the Arctic—these are only names that different people gave to the part of the ocean they knew. The one great ocean covers most of the world. Asia, Africa, North America, and all the other big chunks of land, which are called continents and on which the people of the world live, are really large islands in the one big ocean.

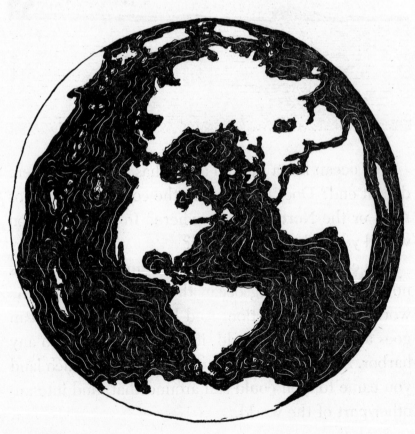

The ocean, like all other things, keeps changing, too. Sometimes the surface is calm, while at other times the waves are high and breakers come smashing against the shore. And you already know about another change. You know that the ocean is slowly becoming saltier and more full of minerals as the rivers keep pouring in their loads of salt and other dissolved materials.

Down at the bottom of the ocean another change is going on all the time. The ocean bottom is gradually being filled up. Every minute of the day and night, a steady rain of tiny particles keeps settling softly on the bottom, heaping up layer on top of layer. What are these particles that keep sifting down all the time?

They are of several kinds. While rivers drop most of the light particles of sand and soil which they are carrying when they enter the ocean, some of the lightest material still remains afloat and is carried many miles out to sea, settling slowly all the time.

But the steady rain of tiny particles that keeps filling up the ocean bottom is mostly a rain of skeletons! All along the surface of the ocean there live tiny animals and plants, so small that a quart of sea water contains millions of them. These tiny animals and plants are of many different shapes and sizes, but most of them are alike in one way—they have hard little skeletons. These tiny creatures live on the surface of the ocean, but when they die their soft parts break away and their hard skeletons sink slowly down to the bottom of the sea.

Although these skeletons are tiny, they keep dropping down in vast numbers, millions of them every day on each square foot of ocean bottom. And other skeletons keep falling down, too—the skeletons of fish and other sea animals that have died or been eaten.

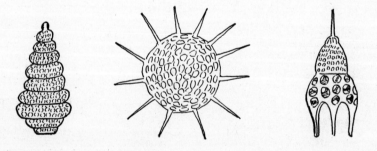

These tiny animal skeletons are shown here thousands of times larger than they really are.

This rain of skeletons has been going on for millions of years, so that by now there are parts of the ocean bottom where the layer of skeletons is over ten thousand feet thick.

The ocean bottom is also being filled up by another material—the ash from volcanoes. Throughout the world, there are about four hundred volcanoes that every once in a while fling huge clouds of fine ash high up into the air. Most of the world's volcanoes are located near the ocean, so that much of the fine ash that is thrown into the air falls into the water. This ash then sinks to the bottom in a soft, steady stream.

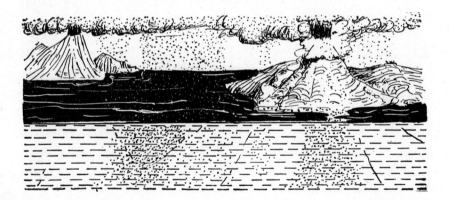

The piling up never stops. The skeletons, big, little, and tiny, keep heaping up. The volcanoes of the world keep pouring out clouds of fine ash. The rivers keep pouring in tons and tons of sand and soil every second. Bit by bit, the ocean bottom is filling up.

When The Ocean Fills Up

Well, what will happen as the ocean bottom keeps rising? Will it just flood the beaches and coastlines? Will it matter to people who don't live near the shore? Here's an experiment that will give you some idea of what can happen as the ocean bed continues to fill up.

EXPERIMENT. You will need: a baking dish, sand enough to half fill it, a cup, a sheet of paper, and water.

Do this: pack the sand in a slanting position, as in the picture. Place the sheet of paper against the sand and then slowly pour in water until the dish is about half full. (The sheet of paper will keep the sand from being washed into the water.) Then carefully slide out the paper. With a crayon, make a mark at the water level on the side of the dish.

Now you are ready to do a little world-changing. The sand in your baking dish will be the land and the water will be the ocean. First make some waves by splashing the "ocean" with your hand. You will see the sand at the shoreline wash away and slide into the water.

102

Along the shorelines of the world, too, the waves are cutting away the land and sliding it into the sea. The material sinks down and adds to the ocean bottom, just as it did at the bottom of the dish.

Now let's do something about rivers in your baking dish.

Do this: with your cup, dip up water from the ocean and pour it on the land at its highest point.

You will find that the sand is washed away and is carried out into the water. Here it sinks to the bottom. Try it with a few cupfuls.

Now look at the water level mark that you made at the beginning of the experiment.

You will find that the ocean in your dish is now *higher* than when you began. You have the same *amount* of water as when you began, but the level is now higher.

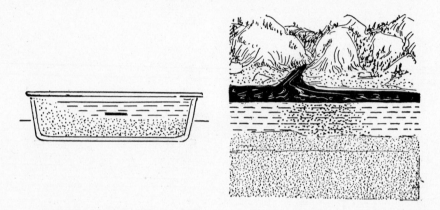

In the same way, when the ocean bottom heaps up with dropped material, it makes the ocean rise, too, even though the amount of water remains about the same.

Now look at your land. You will find that the land is *less steep* than when you began, and there is *less land* showing above the water. Even though you have the same amount of sand as when you began, *most of it is now under water*.

104

The same things that happened in the baking dish are happening in the real world. Rivers are cutting at the high parts of the land, and carrying them down.

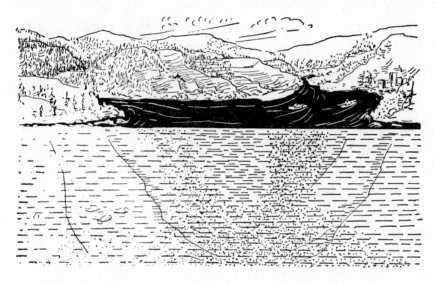

Rivers keep cutting down the land and carrying it to the ocean.

Ocean waves are cutting and hammering away at the shorelines. A good part of this land material is being carried out into the ocean and sinking to the bottom. The ocean bottom is being heaped up with all this material, and with volcano dust and animal skeletons. As this heaping up continues, the water is lifted higher and flows further over the land, so that there is less dry land and more ocean.

Will The World Drown?

What will happen if this keeps on, year after year? Will the world some day be mostly ocean, with just a few high peaks still sticking out as little islands here and there? Will all the people of the world be left huddling together on the remaining bits of land?

You needn't worry about it at all. In the first place, the wearing away of the land is a very, very slow process. It would take millions and millions of years for the land to be worn down to sea level. Secondly, even though the land is being worn down, another process is going on that causes the exact opposite to happen. The land is being built up.

PART THREE
The Land Built Up

Oceans On Top Of Mountains

What is going to build the land up and keep the world from drowning? To find our answer let's go on a voyage of exploration far away from the ocean. Let's take an imaginary trip to the top of a high mountain.

We will need with us a hammer, a chisel, a microscope, and a guide. Our guide is a *geologist,* that is, a scientist who has studied the earth's story. When we reach the top of the mountain let's look at the rocks. At first there seems nothing special about those rocks ex-

LIBRARY

cept that they seem to be arranged in bands, one on top of the other, like a layer cake.

These rocks are rather soft as rocks go, so we can split them easily with a hammer and chisel. If we keep patiently splitting and looking, we may soon come on some things that definitely don't grow on mountain tops. Inside the layers of rocks we may find snail shells, oyster shells, and even the imprint of seaweed. If we are lucky we may even find a fish skeleton.

"Perhaps," you may say, "somebody had a fish picnic up here, and didn't clean up afterwards." But the geologist shows us something else.

Under his microscope some of the powdered rock shows grains of sand and similar material. In addition, there are things that look like the things in the picture.

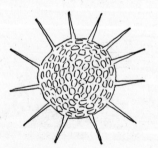

These things are the skeletons of tiny plants and animals that live *only* in the ocean. Under no condition do they ever live on land. Yet here are their skeletons, millions of them in a thimbleful of crushed rock, high up on top of a mountain, a hundred miles from the nearest ocean. How did they get here?

The Riddle

How did the oyster shells, fish skeletons, and grains of sand get on a mountain top? If we keep exploring on our mountain, we will find some clues. For example, some of the rocks when we split them open show wavy marks. These marks look just like the ripples at the bottom of a muddy shore, or a mud flat at low tide.

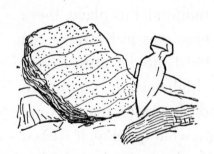 

It would seem as if all this material had once been under water. But how could rippled mud at the bottom of the sea have turned to rippled rock high up on a mountain?

111

The answers were not easy to find. It took many years of study by many scientists all over the world to find a reasonable answer. Our mountain is not very unusual. Geologists found such sea remains on mountains in many parts of the world. And they tried to find out why.

Of course, nobody can be absolutely certain about something no one saw happen. But from the clues you have read about and from thousands of other explorations, geologists are now practically certain that they know how the mountain top was formed long ago, at the bottom of the ocean and how it later rose to where it is now. This is what they believe happened.

The Answer To The Riddle

Millions of years ago, in this mountainous place, there were no mountains at all. There was just a huge sea that covered a large part of the United States. Rivers poured into this sea from the higher land, bringing in sand and mud which settled slowly to the bottom. Where the current flowed somewhat quickly, it stirred the mud into rippled shapes. In this sea, fish and other sea animals lived. And so did sea plants of all shapes and sizes. When these animals and plants died, they sank to the sea bottom and were covered with the sand and mud that drifted down on top of them.

112

Sediment

All this material that settled to the bottom is called *sediment*. Year after year, for millions of years, the bottom kept heaping up with sand and mud, and with the remains of the plant and animal life of the sea. After many centuries the sea bottom was heaped thousands of feet thick with sediment.

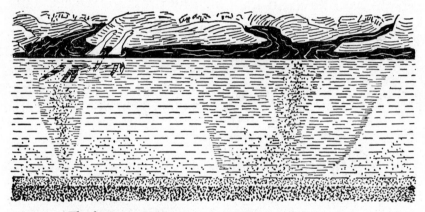

The bottom of the ocean is piled high with sediment.

The heaping up did not go on at a steady rate, however. Sometimes there would be a period of many years of heavy rainfall. The rivers would pour in great quantities of sediment and build up thick layers on the sea bottom. In times of little rainfall, the rivers just trickled in, adding very little material to the sea bottom. In this way, the sea bottom was built up in layers of uneven thickness, one layer at a time. And as it built up, something kept happening to all this sediment.

113

Sediment Under Pressure

What happened was that these layers were squeezed slowly and steadily for millions of years by the weight of the water and other layers of material on top of them. The bottom layers, of course, were squeezed the most. If you have ever made snowballs, or sandballs, by squeezing the snow or sand very, very tightly into shape, you have an idea of how pressure works. This squeezing was one of the reasons the sand and mud at the bottom of the ocean hardened and stuck together.

 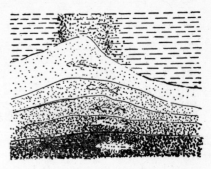

The sticking-together process was helped along by some of the dissolved minerals brought in by the river water. Many soils have minerals in them that act as a kind of cement. The plaster on your walls, for example, comes from a dry powdery mineral in the ground. It changes into a smooth, firm, surface material after it is spread on the wall. Clay is another kind of soil that dries into something like stone. It becomes strong enough to be used for cooking pots or dishes. Even when it is used as a water jug it does not become soft. Cement, itself, is a fine, soft, powdery thing when you get it in the sack. But when it is mixed with sand, water, and pebbles it changes into strong, hard concrete, used for building roads, bridges, and houses.

In such a way, the dissolved minerals brought in by the river water helped change the sediment. These minerals acted as a kind of cement. Working together for millions of years, the cement-like minerals and the squeezing caused the layers of sediment, sand, shells, skeletons, and mud to harden into layers of rock. And because this rock was formed out of sediment, it is called *sedimentary rock.*

Sedimentary Rock

You don't have to go to the mountains to find sedimentary rock that was once at the bottom of the sea. No matter where you live, you can almost certainly find some. Railroad lines and highways are often cut right through sloping land in order to make them as level as possible. In such cut-through places, you can find sedimentary rock in layers. In level country, you can find cut-through places along the banks of rivers or where cellars are being dug for new buildings.

If you see rock arranged in layers, then you know it is sedimentary rock and that the land you are standing on was once at the bottom of the sea.

Sea Bottom In Use

When you go for a walk, or take a trip, watch for the bands and layers of rock that tell you the story of a long stay at the bottom of the sea and then of a journey up. All around us, every day, we see and use materials that geologists have found were once at the bottom of the sea. There are many that you can see for yourself.

116

If you happen to be reading this in a school class-room, you probably have a large slab of ocean-bottom rock staring you in the face—the blackboard. Many blackboards are made of *slate*, which was formed millions of years ago at the bottom of lakes and seas.

Slate comes from clay which has very tiny particles, much smaller than sand grains. The clay particles were brought in by rivers, settled to the bottom along with other sediment, and were then pressed and cemented into a soft sedimentary rock called *shale*. Still more pressure changed the soft shale into hard slate.

In the same way, the mud that you stir up when you go swimming in a brook may become the blackboard cut out of a mountain for use in a schoolroom a million years from now!

Ocean bottom of long ago becomes today's blackboard.

The piece of chalk that you write with on the blackboard is also sedimentary material. Most chalk is made by cutting pieces out of chalk mountains, such as the chalk cliffs of Dover, England. These high white cliffs are made of billions of tiny sea-animal skeletons, packed closely together.

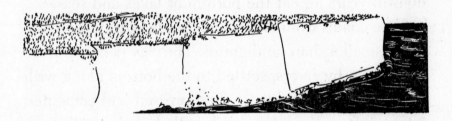

Sedimentary Rock In Buildings

Not only chalk and blackboards, but most large buildings are built of rock made of layers of sand, mud, and animal skeletons—all sedimentary materials. The outside walls of your post office or library may be made of *sandstone*. Even though it is dug out of a mountainside, sandstone often contains seashells and the skeletons of sea animals.

The walls of the building may be of *limestone*, another kind of stone dug out of mountains. Yet this is stone that was formed, like chalk, mostly out of shells and sea-animal skeletons. The skeletons and shells which make up limestone are harder and heavier than chalk. There are many buildings in Texas, as well as in other places, where you can clearly see shells embedded in the limestone.

118

Iron

The iron that is used in so many ways all around you also comes from ocean beds. You know that river water carries dissolved minerals. Iron we use today was dissolved out of rocks and soil and brought down by rivers and deposited on the ocean bottom. Now, ages later, it is dug out of mines high above the sea.

There is another more curious way that we get our supply of iron. Certain very tiny water bacteria left it for us. These bacteria have very special food tastes. They actually take in dissolved iron from the water as food and then give off pure iron as the waste product of digestion. It is hard to believe that tiny bacteria can build iron deposits as waste material, but it's true. This is another part of the almost incredible story of earth's changes.

From the rock came the iron dissolved in water. It was carried into the ocean, taken in as food by bacteria, given off as waste, and put down to make rocky beds of iron again. And ages later, it was dug out of mines to be used by people.

Fuel

The coal, oil, or gas used for heating your building came from the bottom of the sea, too. Each was formed in its own way.

Coal was formed out of plants that grew in swamps millions of years ago. The plants grew, died, and sank into the swamps. Other plants grew on top of them, and still others, year after year. After a time there was a thick layer of rotting plant material. Then the swamp and the land around it sank slowly, until finally it was covered by water. Over the plant layer there piled up layers of sediment that gradually turned into sedimentary rock. The plant material, squeezed by the weight of the rock and the water above it, changed into coal. The layers of old plant material are the coal deposits. Today, people dig coal out of these ancient

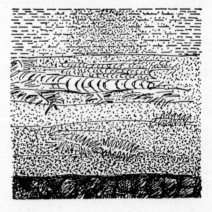

Swamp plants of long ago are the coal of today.

sea bottoms that are now part of the land. In stoves and furnaces, the coal burns and gives off heat that was stored in it when the sun shone on plants millions of years ago.

The best coal is the hardest. It is called *anthracite,* and it is found in places that have had the greatest pressure on top of the plant material. Soft coal was formed under less pressure. *Peat* is coal that is just beginning to form.

Oil, too, was formed in ancient seas long ago, although the exact process is not known. Scientists believe that oil was made out of the bodies of sea animals, and perhaps plants, that died and sank to the sand at the bottom of the sea. There they were covered with layers of sediment that turned into sedimentary rock. The pressure of the rock and sea water on top of them changed some of the dead material into oil that oozed out and collected in the porous sand. Today,

121

millions of years after the process first began, the oil is pumped up through holes that have been drilled through the rock layers. Then in oil refineries it is cleaned and changed into gasoline, lubricating oil, paraffin, asphalt, and many other useful products.

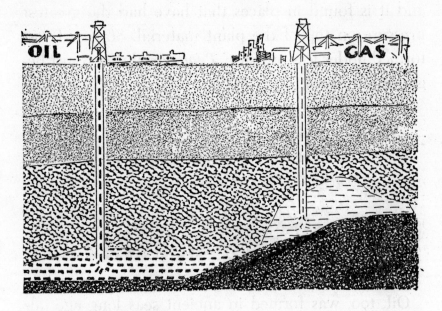

Whenever oil is formed, gas usually collects too. It collects in empty spaces, or pockets in the rocks above the oil. When oil wells are drilled, the gas is sent through pipes to nearby cities, to be used as a fuel for cooking and house-heating. This kind of gas is called *natural gas*. Another kind of gas is made by heating coal or oil. Both kinds really began at the bottom of the sea.

122

You And The Bottom Of The Sea

Last, but not least, *you* are part of that magic journey from the bottom of the sea. Part of you was once part of the ocean. Your bones and teeth, for example, are made mostly of a mineral called *calcium.*

When this calcium lay at the bottom of the sea, it was the material that formed several billion tiny animal skeletons. Over the centuries, these skeletons were weighted down and compressed into chalk or limestone. Then the sea bottom rose up and became dry land with chalk and limestone in it. These soft stones weathered and crumbled and turned into part of the soil.

Ages later, a farmer planted some seeds in this crumbled-down limestone soil. Then the seeds, as they grew into ripe plants, drew up some calcium through their roots. When you ate the plant, the calcium was used by your body for building teeth and bones. The calcium went a long way from the bottom of the sea to get to your teeth, and it took a long time getting there —several million years.

Teeth and bones are not the only parts of you made out of ancient sedimentary rock. The red color of your blood comes from iron. When you blush, it's ancient sedimentary iron showing in your cheeks. Your blood contains large amounts of iron that came from the soil through the plants you ate, or by way of meat from animals that had eaten plants. That iron was once sea-bottom material.

Other minerals in your body came from the sea. The salt you need and sprinkle on your food comes from salt mines. These were once shallow seas from which the water evaporated, leaving the salt behind. To be a healthy person you need other minerals, too. *Iodine, phosphorus, sulphur, copper, potassium* are the names of some of these minerals, which like salt, have all made that long-distance, long-time journey from the bottom of the sea to you.

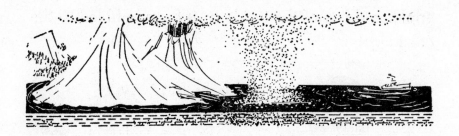

The Ups And Downs
Of The Earth

High up on the mountains, we find many things that have been formed at the bottom of the sea. Coal and marble, chalk and iron, slate and salt, and many more everyday things have made that long journey from the ocean to high above sea level. All the clues seem to point to the fact that, in many places in the world, the bottom of the sea was moved or lifted thousands of feet high. How did it get there?

Geologists have worked out two chief answers to the puzzling question of how the earth's surface can move.

The Answer Of The Baked Apple

You have seen an apple before and after baking. A fresh, firm apple with a smooth tightly fitting skin looks quite different after an hour or so in a hot oven. After baking, the skin is all wrinkled and bumpy. There are holes and cracks in various parts of the apple, and bits of the inside fruit have bubbled to the outside.

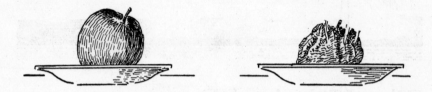

There is a lot of water in the fruit of an apple. During baking, this water steams and bubbles and puffs out of the apple and evaporates. As the water escapes, the inside becomes smaller. As the inside shrinks, the skin caves in and falls into folds and wrinkles.

The earth, too, is hot inside—much, much hotter than any baked apple. Just as a hot baked apple puffs out juice and bits of apple, so the huge earth puffs out bits of molten material and steam from very deep inside it. Every time a volcano erupts, it flings out tons and tons of hot gases, steam, and molten rocks from deep inside the earth.

So we do know that the inside of the earth is definitely becoming smaller, because of the material being forced out through volcanoes. As the inside becomes smaller, the earth's crust settles down to fill up the hollow spaces. It settles into wrinkles and folds like those on the baked apple. On the earth's wrinkled crust or "skin," the high places make mountains, the low places make valleys, and the lowest places sea bottoms. As these boilings and steamings and bubblings continue in the earth, with heating and cooling in different parts, new wrinkles and hollows appear. In this way high lands sink into the hollows between wrinkles to become ocean beds, and sea bottoms wrinkle up and rise to form new mountains.

This is one explanation of how the earth's surface changes its shape—how low places are lifted and high places sink down.

The Answer Of The Toothpaste Tube

You can find another answer in a toothpaste tube. If you have a half-empty tube of toothpaste in the house, try this simple experiment.

Experiment. Do this: place the tube on a flat surface and then squeeze it until the whole tube is flat and even. Then press down on the rear half with your fist.

You will find that the front half of the tube will fill and rise. It was pushed up by the paste that flowed over from the rear half.

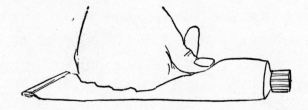

What does this show? From this you can see that when you squeeze *down* at one place, you can cause material to flow *away* from there and *up* into another place where the squeeze is less.

In this experiment, the material, toothpaste, was soft and easy to push. If the tube had been half filled with candle wax, you would have had to push much harder and longer, but the wax would have moved, although very slowly, in the same way that the toothpaste did.

And here's something hard to believe, but scientists have found it true by many actual experiments. If the tube had been filled with steel or hard rock, the results would have been the same! A much greater squeeze would have been necessary, and it would have taken a very much longer time, but the material, no matter how tough, would gradually have flowed away from the place of greater squeeze over and up into the place of lesser squeeze.

How does the answer of the toothpaste tube help explain the movement of the earth's surface? You already know that rivers are constantly grinding away land material and carrying it out into the ocean. Every

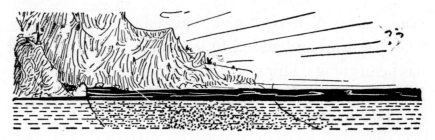

Slowly, as the mainland is worn down, the ocean bed heaps up.

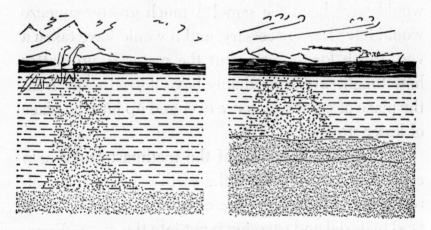

Slowly, as islands are worn down, the ocean bed heaps up.

year billions of tons of rock and sediment are taken from the land and added to the ocean bed. And this has been going on for many millions of years. Gradually the land has become lighter and the ocean bed has become heavier.

130

As the ocean bed gets heavier, and the land gets lighter, the pressure on the rock layers under the ocean becomes much greater than on the rock layers under the land. Let's remember that pressure causes any material, no matter how hard, to flow. And just as it did in the toothpaste tube, it always flows *from* the greater squeeze *toward* the lesser squeeze.

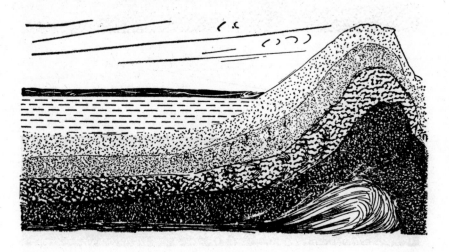

So here we have rock layers deep down under the ocean being squeezed with greater and greater force as the ocean beds pile up with material brought from the land. Under this enormous pressure, scientists believe, the rock layers under the ocean gradually flowed away from the squeeze to surge upward at a place of lesser squeeze. You can see how this would deepen some places and raise others.

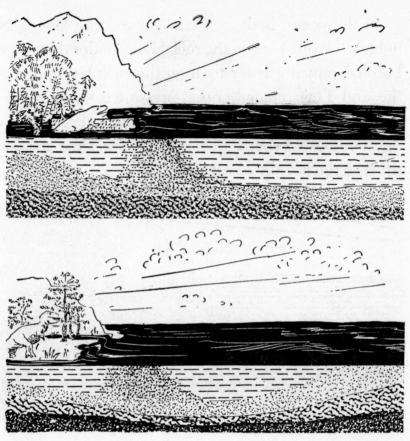

As the land is carried into the sea, the sea bottom becomes heavier.

In this way, land that has been worn and washed down by rivers is pushed up once again. The sediment increases the weight of the ocean bottom. The added pressure causes the earth materials to flow away toward another place. Slowly, slowly, less than an inch a year, the wearing down of the earth is balanced by a surging up.

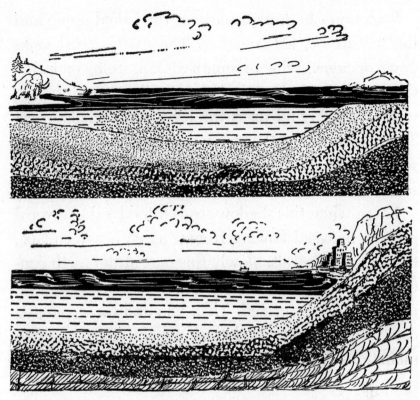

The heavier sea bottom increases the downward pressure
and raises part of the land.

Of course, this movement up and down goes on over great stretches of time. Over millions and millions of years, highlands and mountains are gradually worn down and become lighter. Slowly, slowly, the sea bottom heaps up heavier and heavier with the enormous weight of the sediment and rock. Over countless ages, the lowlands are slowly raised into highlands and mountains.

133

LIBRARY

Sometimes both explanations, the baked apple and the toothpaste, act together. The earth's crust sinks down or caves in due to some shrinking going on inside the earth. The land sinks below sea level, and the sea water flows in and turns the land into a shallow sea. Then sediment, with its sea skeletons and shells and seaweed, and perhaps strange fish, settles on this new sea bottom.

Later, when this shallow sea is lifted by the upward push of material flowing from a much heavier place, the water drains off. Slowly this part of the earth continues to be raised and a mountain with layers of sedimentary rock is formed. Then you and the geologists can find deep-sea skeletons on the tops of high mountains.

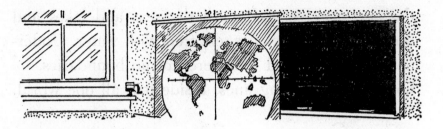

The Earth Inside

A map of the earth is a quiet-looking thing, with its great stretches of calm blue sea, and its pretty colored lands. The continents and islands seem to be curled and curving pieces of land floating in the ocean. The mountain chains are like fences built on top of the level land. But the real earth is not like that.

The real earth is one earth; one heavy, hard, tremendous globe. All the islands and continents and mountains are just slightly higher ridges and rises of

135

the one massive globe. All the seas and lakes and oceans are lower places, covered with water. Underneath the land and sea there are no boundaries, no borders, no dividing lines. Inside it is all one world.

Under the ocean, Europe, Africa, Asia, and Australia are all connected to each other and to the United States. The oceans that seem to divide the land are only big lakes.

What is the earth like inside? No one has ever gone through the dense, solid mass of earth from one side to the other. But geologists have done thousands of explorations. They have climbed deep down into mines. They have lowered cameras to the ocean floor and plunged instruments down, too, to crawl along the bottom like crabs. They have peered into volcanoes and thumped and listened to the earth's surface like doctors thumping your chest. And they have found out two important things.

Under the cities and farms, under the rivers and

ocean, straight through 8,000 miles to the other side, the earth is made of hard rock and metals. That's the first thing.

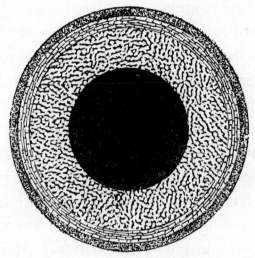

Scientists believe that the center of the earth is made up of fiery hot liquid rock and metals. Outside is a crust of cooled rock.

And the second thing is that deep down inside the earth it is very, very hot. The heat is so great that it can melt the rock and mineral materials.

These two things—the heavy earth materials and the terrific heat deep down below the surface—cause many changes in the world up above. Some of these changes are very slow, while others are violent, sudden and exciting. And the story of these changes is written in the rocks everywhere.

Magma

Underneath, down deep inside the earth, the great heat melts the rock and metals. Such melted or molten rock is called *magma*.

This terrifically hot magma has played a big part in the earth's story of endless change. Just as water, wind, heat and cold have changed the earth from the outside, so magma has changed the shape of the earth's crust from the inside.

It has pushed and piled up mountains, and built islands. It has split great cracks and poked holes in the earth. It has poured gold and silver and precious metals into some cracks and plugged some holes with diamonds. The inside of the earth is constantly changing the outside. Right this very minute magma is changing the world.

What Magma Does

The hot magma doesn't remain still. Pressed under the enormous weight of the earth above it, the great hot mass moves very, very slowly. Wherever it can

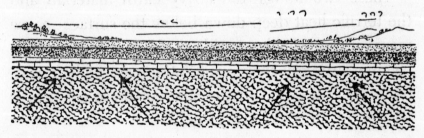

find a weak spot, a crack, or a softer place, this molten rock substance oozes up.

Wherever magma moves up, it makes great changes. Where magma moves, it shifts the crust of the earth that is above it. The layers of rock and surface soil move with the movement of magma.

Folded Mountains

The earth's crust doesn't *usually* crack when it moves. Usually, the movements are very, very slow, so that the rock layers of the crust have time to move slowly, too, bit by bit, to their new position. As the magma presses against the outer layers, they bend into long wave-like curves. These curves may be gentle, in which case the landscape will show low rolling hills and wide rounded valleys. Or the curves may be greater, so that the crust is bent into high, rounded mountains and narrow valleys.

If you live near hills or mountains, you can tell whether they were formed by a curving of the earth's

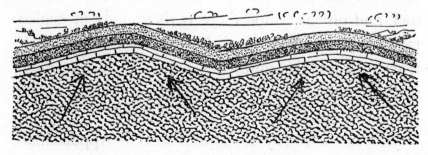

crust. Just find a place where a railroad or road has been cut through a hill and look at the exposed rock layers. If the layers of sedimentary rock are curved in the same shape as the mountain, then you are looking at a portion of the earth's crust that was bent from a flat position into a curved shape. This is called a *folded mountain.*

Very often, when rocks are bent into the shape of folded mountains, a space is left inside. The space becomes filled with magma that flows up from deep inside the earth. This magma, when it cools, turns to rock, so that the mountain is made of two kinds of rock. On the outside there is sedimentary, or layered, rock and on the inside there is rock made of cooled magma. This magma rock is called *igneous rock.* It is easy to tell the difference between igneous rocks and sedimentary rocks because igneous rocks are *not* formed in layers.

Most of the Rocky Mountains and the Appalachian

140

Mountains were made as folded mountains. First, level sedimentary layers of rock were pushed up, and slowly flowing magma filled the hollow spaces. Then the magma cooled into hard, igneous rock. In this way moving magma slowly and powerfully pushed up the earth's surface and made some of the mountains.

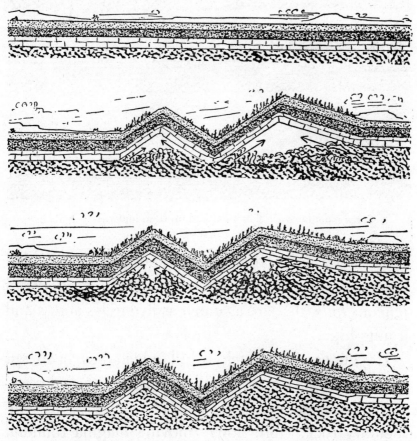

Sometimes the flat crust of the earth buckles and heaves up.
A new mountain is made!

Igneous Hills

Sometimes magma oozes up with greater force, or the underneath layers of soil and rock are weak. In such places the magma breaks its way through several layers down below, and then, with some push still left, it

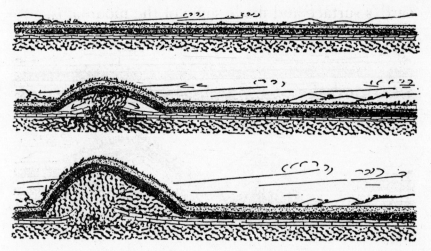

Some mountains are slowly pushed up from underneath by hot magma.

will heave the remaining layers above it into rounded dome-shaped hills. There are hills of this type, called *igneous hills*, that are as much as five miles across and a mile high.

If you can find such a hill which has been cut through to make a road, you can see the core of once-molten rock covered by a coat of many-layered sedimentary rock. Here slowly moving magma rounded the earth's surface into hills.

142

Volcanoes

What happens when magma under high pressure comes to a crack or a weak place in the earth's crust? You can figure it out for yourself from the baked apple. The magma pours out of the earth in a molten stream called *lava*. Wherever lava pours out of the earth, you have a volcano. Volcanoes are just holes

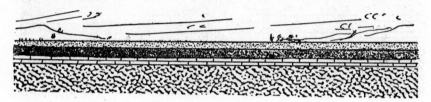

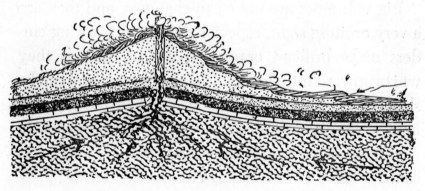

This is what happens when hot magma, pushing up, finds a
weak spot in the earth's crust.

out of which magma pours from the inside layers of the earth to the surface. Volcanoes have different sizes and shapes and mixtures and pressures, but each kind of volcano changes the earth's shape in its own way.

143

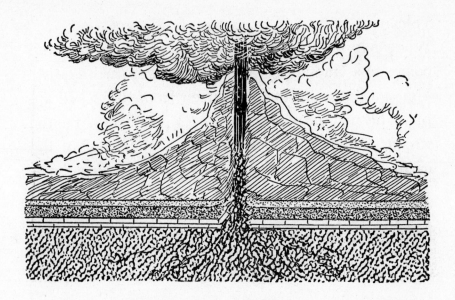

Big volcanoes are big earth-changers, and they are a very exciting sight, especially at night. Glowing cinders make brilliant orange streaks of light as they whizz upward into the sky. Clouds of steam and smoke shine in the yellow and orange light of the glowing lava, welling and bubbling out of the volcano's mouth. And the lava itself, as it flows down the side of the volcano, is like a river of many-colored fire.

The fiery lava flows along for a while and then slows down. As it cools, it forms solid, igneous rock. Gradually, these rocks and cinders are heaped up into a cone-shaped mountain with a hollow tube through its center, out of which pours smoke, steam, and gas, mixed with molten mineral material. As more and

144

more molten material pours out of the volcano's center, the lava spreads and covers fields and towns for miles around the volcano. And since a volcano may remain active for many years, there are places where the beds of solid lava are over ten thousand feet thick.

Think of the changes that took place as thick layers of the earth's magma, heavy with all kinds of minerals and metals, piled up on the surface of the earth! Where the lava had a bubbling foam surface, full of air and gases, the volcanic rock into which it cooled is light and porous. This kind of rock is *pumice stone,* which is used in many cleansing powders. When next you scrub something with cleansing powder, you will know that there in your hand is a bit of foam that bubbled out of the deepest inside of the earth through a fiery volcano.

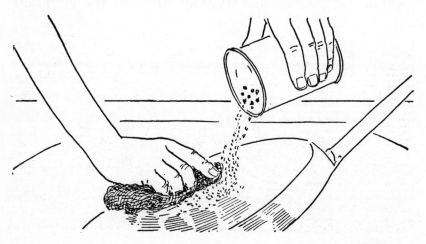

There are about 400 active volcanoes in the world, and occasionally a new one pops up. But this generally happens in places where there are other volcanoes already present. It happened not so long ago (in 1943) in Mexico. A farmer noticed smoke and steam puffing up from the ground in his corn field. Soon lava began to pour out, and within a few days there was a mountain of lava several hundred feet high. Seven years later, this young volcano, called Paricutin, was almost a mile high. It keeps on growing, but it is beginning to slow down. Magma has changed the shape of the earth. It built a high mountain on top of a level field.

Volcanoes Out Of The Ocean

Sometimes volcanoes pop up out of the bottom of the ocean. Magma breaks its way through the sedimen-

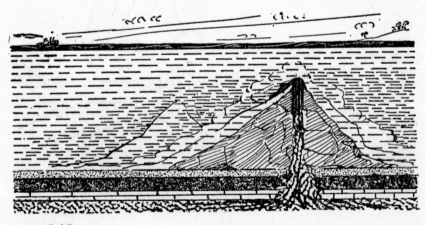

146

tary rock layers on the ocean's floor and begins to pour out, forming a volcano that grows and grows under the water. There are whole mountains under the sea that were formed in this way. Sometimes the volcano grows until its top may even reach above the ocean. Volcanic islands were formed this way, out of magma that flowed up through a volcano on the bottom of the ocean and hardened into igneous rock.

The Hawaiian Islands grew in this way. These islands are now large enough to have cities and villages with many people living in them, even though the volcano, Mauna Lao, occasionally still erupts. It is less and less active, and perhaps it will not be very long before the pressure that forces up the magma in this area will die out. Then Mauna Loa will be a quiet, high, snow-covered mountain like many other old, extinct volcanoes.

More Volcanoes

Sometimes the shape of a volcano is not so exciting as an ocean island or a mountain cone. Sometimes lava pours out of a long crack in the earth instead of through a single opening. Then it spreads out over a vast area. This was more common, geologists say, many, many millions of years ago. Along the West Coast, in the states of Oregon and Washington, the layers of old lava are almost a mile thick! Where the rivers have cut through these layers, the deep canyon walls show that all that part of the land is made of the earth's inner magma which poured out over the earth's crust.

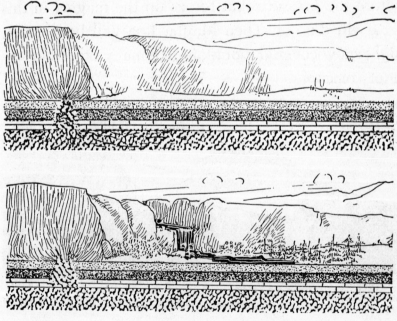

The famous Palisades along the Hudson River were formed when lava oozed up out of a crack in the shape of a dike—a high wall.

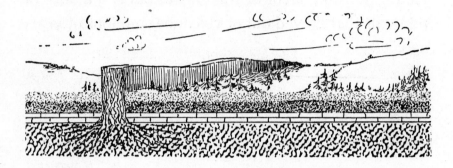

All the boiling, bubbling, and burning sounds as if volcanoes are altogether destructive things. But magma, when it pours out of the earth, brings important gifts. Many of the good and lovely things of the earth are the work of volcanoes.

Lava Into Soil
Rich, fertile fields, like those of Idaho, were once hot lava layers. Volcanoes helped to build the good soil. As it oozed up, magma brought with it many important minerals as well as valuable gases and liquids. These all cooled into igneous rock. Then the wind and the rain began their work. These with the help of lichens, mosses, and other green things weathered down the rocks. In this way, the rich lava particles

slowly became part of the soil. In the soil they are ready for plants to draw them up for food. As plants, they are ready to be used by birds and beasts and men. The good flavor of Idaho potatoes is the taste of minerals that flowed out of volcanoes millions of years ago.

Lava from inside the earth adds to the flavor of your food.

Much of the world's land was raised from under the sea by magma. It was piled up as islands, fields, and mountains by magma pouring out of volcanoes.

Precious Stones

Some volcanoes produced precious jewels. The fiercely hot center core of cinders and ashes cooled into a kind of treasure chest. Sometimes diamonds were formed here in the fiery magma like soot on the walls of a fireplace. These diamonds began in the deep layers of the earth, in rock and metal which was molten and which rose as vapor and ash in a volcano. When it cooled, this material hardened into a column filled with precious stones. Then other movements of the magma lowered this volcanic core into the earth. Ages later these stones were mined from their bed of blue and yellow mineral powder. After they are cut and polished, they shine like fire caught in ice with their own blue, green, yellow, orange, or blue-white glow.

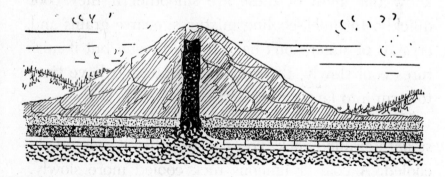

Precious Metals

In the process of cooling, magma left deposits of gold, silver, and other metals in the cracks of rocks. These minerals, that bubbled and boiled up from the earth's inside, cooled and hardened on the rock layers. Here, deposited as veins in mines, we are sometimes able to get at the treasure that volcanoes have poured out of the inner earth.

All Kinds of Igneous Rock

Not all cooled magma becomes diamonds or other precious jewels and metals. But it all cools and becomes hard. All cooled magma is called igneous rock, because igneous means fire-formed rock. The special kind of rock it becomes depends upon the kind of magma that formed it. How the rock looks depends on what was "cooked" in it and how long it cooled.

If you have ever made ice cream or fudge, you know that both of these are smoother if they cool quickly. In quick-cooling mixtures, coarse grains and crystals of sugar don't have time to form; but if mixtures cool slowly, the grains separate and have time to form into larger particles.

The same is true of igneous rock. If you see a smooth-grained rock, you can tell that it was quick-cooled. A coarser igneous rock cooled more slowly.

Igneous rocks may be of practically any color, depending on the particles that were cooked in them. They may be red, blue, brown, yellow, spotted, speck-

152

led, dull, or shiny. They may have particles of quartz-like glass or gleaming mica-like bits of mirror. They may be colored with flecks of gold, silver, rainbow opals, or grains of cinder-black. The loveliest bits and colors are used for jewels.

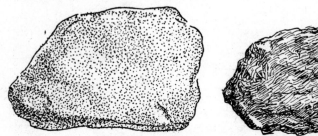

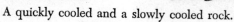
A quickly cooled and a slowly cooled rock.

One of the most common and useful rocks—not as precious as diamond, but much more valuable to the world—is granite. This is a hard, long-lasting rock, that weathers well without crumbling when it is used in buildings. When it is used for statues and monuments, it polishes smoothly and well, and is often very beautiful with its flecks of various colors. When it remains in the ground, it weathers slowly, giving up important minerals that enrich the soil.

A rock that cooled very much more quickly than granite, and left no time for grains or crystals to form, is called *obsidian*. It is smooth and clear like shiny dark glass. It is usually black, but sometimes it is dark red or green. People long ago used obsidian to make

153

sharp, hard arrowheads or knives. There are magnificent, huge chunks of obsidian mountain in the Indian country of western United States.

Granite, diamonds, silver, gold, obsidian, lead, the minerals we need for the soil, the rocks and palisades and hills and mountains—all these and other treasures are blown and thrown and poured and flung to us from deep inside of the earth.

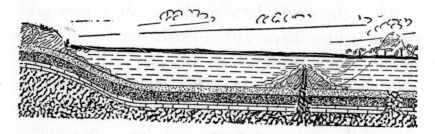

The Earth Inside And Out

You have seen that magma from the inside of the earth will force its way up against the earth's crust, lifting hills, pouring out of volcanoes, heaping up islands, piling up rocks, changing the earth's surface in many ways.

There are other kinds of changes caused by flowing magma. Sometimes as it flows, it leaves the earth above it unsupported. As the magma shifts its position, the earth's surface does too.

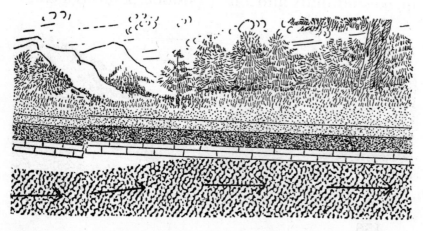

When the earth shifts suddenly into a new position, it settles down with a crash. This is an earthquake. Some earthquakes are only felt as slight tremors, but some are big. They shake the mountains and tip the rocks into new positions. Earthquakes can change the course of rivers, and they may empty a lake, or create a waterfall. In the ocean, an earthquake may cause a huge wave that washes over the land suddenly. This is called a *tidal wave*. In a city, an earthquake may topple over buildings as it heaves up the earth.

Fortunately these big sudden movements of the earth's crust come very seldom, and only at certain few places on the earth.

A Fault
When the earth's crust gives way during an earthquake and shifts into a new position, it forms a crack,

called a *fault*. The land on both sides of the fault may settle along the crack and change level land into steeply sloping land. Or the land may settle straight down into the crack, and a steep cliff will be formed.

If a river has been flowing along this land, the river's appearance also changes. The water now pours from the higher land to the lower land in a waterfall. Many waterfalls were formed in this way, as the result of a shifting of the earth's crust.

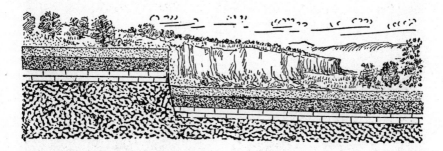

Suppose the gradually sloping land is shaken in the opposite way, so that the higher part of the land slips down. Now it has become the lower part. The river

157

LIBRARY

can't very well jump up from its lowered position. Instead, it flows in and heaps up until it has formed a lake. The lake fills up higher and higher, flooding the

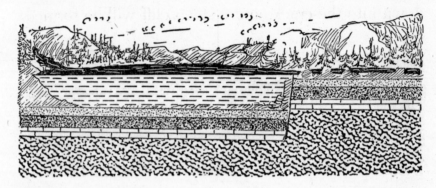

land behind it. When the water in the lake is heaped high enough, it overflows and continues on its new way. If the cliff is too high, the river will find another way downhill and make a river where no river was before.

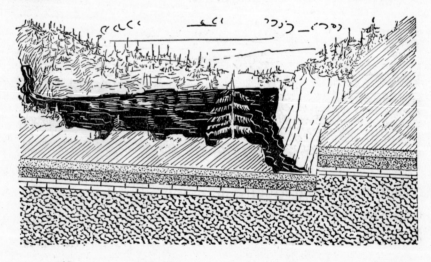

Many great earth changes have been made by these sudden earthquake movements of the earth's crust. When the movement caused a sudden tilting of the rock layers, fault mountains were formed. Cliffs, waterfalls, and lakes were formed, too, whenever the earth's crust changed its position. And all these movements of magma are still going on. The sudden shifts and the slow pressures, together, built all the great mountain systems of the world, and they continue building more mountains and valleys in many parts of the world.

Magma Meets Water

Sometimes magma, as it forces its way up, meets underground water. Where it does, it shows its presence in an exciting way—steam spouts out of the ground.

One such place is Yellowstone National Park, Wyoming, where there are many of these steam spouts called *geysers*. This is where the famous geyser, Old Faithful, is. Old Faithful spouts a stream of hot water and steam out of the ground high into the air regularly for several minutes of every hour.

Steam shoots high into the air as Old Faithful spouts regularly
every hour.

If you have a percolator in your house, especially a glass one, you can see a geyser in miniature. The steam of the boiling water pushes the water up through the narrow pipe. It bubbles over the coffee grounds and trickles down. It boils up through the pipe and trickles down over the grounds, over and over again.

160

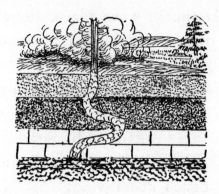

Geologists are reasonably sure that geysers are the result of a meeting between magma and underground water. Underground water, pouring over hot magma, quickly boils and turns into steam. The steam collects in the geyser's crooked pathway through underground rock layers, and, when it has sufficient pressure, shoots up to the surface. Some geysers spout up 150 feet high in the air.

Steam Wells

Sometimes steam does not collect but pours out in a steady stream like the steam out of the spout of a tea

kettle. In some places the steam comes out in such great quantities that it can actually be put to work. In Italy, for example, there is a well from which steam is piped to several powerhouses. There it drives steam engines that turn electric generators. The generators supply electricity for several large cities nearby. And in California, near San Francisco, there are a number of such steam wells.

Hot Springs

Sometimes the flow of water against the hot magma is too great for all the water to be turned into steam. Then the water is heated and continues to flow until it reaches a hole in the earth's crust. The hot water, as it flows, usually dissolves many minerals out of the rocks through which it passes. When it reaches the

162

surface, it is full of dissolved minerals. Warm Springs, Georgia, and Hot Springs, Arkansas, are two of many health and pleasure resorts in the United States that make use of the meeting between magma and underground water. In Iceland, there are hot springs that are used to supply hot water for many homes and public buildings.

Metamorphic Rock

There is still another change in the earth's crust due to magma. Magma is very hot material, much hotter than the inside of a furnace or oven. As it forces its way up over or between the layers of sedimentary rock, it bakes the rock and changes it considerably. This changed rock is called *metamorphic rock*. Metamorphic just means changed in form.

The same kind of change takes place when clay is baked into pottery. The clay, which is sedimentary material, becomes hard, tough, and glassy when baked in a hot kiln. Clay, china, porcelain, and all kinds of crockery dishes and pottery are all made by baking. In the same way, when hot magma flows over or through sedimentary rock, it bakes the rock. The heated rock becomes hard and tough and often has a glassy look.

Baked Rock

Perhaps you have seen buildings which are all or partly made of marble. Banks, post office buildings, museums, and schools often have marble trim or stairways. Marble is a metamorphic rock that began as tiny animal skeletons and seashells that were compressed at the bottom of the sea into soft limestone. Then this sedimentary limestone was squeezed and

164

heated by magma. The pressure and heat turned the limestone into marble of many colors or pure white, depending on the color of the sediment out of which it was originally formed. Black, pink, yellow and red seashells give marble its varied and lovely colors.

Long after it was formed, the marble was lifted by powerful forces—the upward pressure of magma or the weight of sediment on another part of the sea. The beds of marble became mountains of marble. Millions of years later, some of this marble is quarried and polished into blocks of gleaming stone—metamorphic rock that was made by the heat and pressure of magma.

Magma, The Great Earth-Changer

By now you see that there is a steady stream of traffic going on all the time from the inside of the earth to the outside. Steam and hot water spurt out from geysers and hot springs. Magma seeps up into sedimentary rock, baking it into metamorphic rock. Magma pushes up hills, and pours out in enormous quantities through all kinds of volcanoes. It shifts the rocks and slants them into peaks and jags them out in cliffs. It makes high places low and low places high. And all this has been going on for hundreds of millions of years, changing the earth's surface all the time.

PART FOUR
Man And The Earth

The Earth's Story

The story of the earth is everywhere, and everything tells its part. Now you have learned how to read some of that story. Now, when you pick up a pebble or watch a raindrop falling, when you go hiking on a mountain or swimming in a brook, you will see everything as part of the changing earth.

You will see the raindrop as part of the never-ending water cycle. The raindrop is itself for only a moment. It was part of a cloud and part of the sea, it flowed in a mountain brook and seeped through the earth deep underground. Over and over again, the raindrop has made its journeys to the far places of the earth.

The pebble, too, has traveled far and wide. Long ago it was a drop of magma, molten rock that poured out from deep inside the earth. Perhaps when the magma cooled it formed part of a mountain that was later worn down and carried away by a rushing stream. Or the pebble may have been carried thousands of miles by a slowly moving glacier that finally melted and left it there for you to pick up. It has traveled to many places and has been part of many things.

On a walk in the country, you can see the earth's story everywhere around you. A muddy river tells you of unprotected soil farther upstream. The flat layers in a rock tell you that the rock was formed at the bottom of the sea. The curving layers in a rounded hill tell you that the hill was pushed by the pressure of magma underneath, or formed by the wrinkling and bending of the earth's crust. Even in a handful of soil there are bits of mountains, traces of sea ani-

mals, crumbled remains of last year's leaves, and the minerals of plants that lived millions of years ago.

In the city, too, you can see the earth's story all around you. The cement of the sidewalks, the bricks of the chimneys, the plaster of the walls, all come from rock that was broken apart and ground to pieces by wind and water, heat and cold. The wood of the floors and furniture came from trees that drew their minerals out of the rock-formed soil. The copper and iron of the wires and pipes were once magma that flowed up from deep inside the earth.

You are part of the earth's story. In your blood is iron from plants that drew it out of the soil. Your teeth and bones were once coral of the sea and tiny, beautiful sea animals. The water you drink has been in clouds high over the highest mountains of Asia and in lovely, misty waterfalls in Africa. The air you breathe has blown and swirled through places of the earth that no one has ever seen. Every bit of you is a bit of the earth, and has been on many strange and wonderful journeys over countless millions of years.

The story of the earth is in everything, everywhere.

Index

Index

176